I've Seen It All...

Tricks, Tips, Laughs and more!

Sean McCormack

Sean McCormack

This book is dedicated to my Mom...

"POI"

Acknowledgments

I am using this acknowledgments page(s) to thank all of the women that have influenced me to write this book or have impacted my life significantly.

My Wife *– Azure McCormack*

The only reason I began writing in the first place was because of you. I can vividly recall the night I spoke with you about an opportunity to write an article for PHC News Magazine. I had come up with an interesting article idea and reached out to the editor of the magazine. He told me to go ahead and write up the piece and if he liked my writing he would publish the article in the following month's issue. I instantly became nervous about the idea. I didn't think I had the skills or the creativity to write the actual article and have that article published in a major publication. Azure, I remember when you looked at me like I was the craziest person when I told you I wasn't sure if I'd want to write the piece. You encouraged me and gave me the confidence to be able to speak my mind freely and let my creativity flow naturally. You changed my life that evening and now here I am writing this book. I Love you, always and forever. Thank You…

My Mom – *Noreen McCormack*

There isn't a day that goes by that I don't think about you. I know you are looking down on me every day and I can only hope that I bring a smile to your face. There have been so many times in my life since you have left us that I wish I could just hear those words that you whispered in my ear, the night of my wedding when we danced together. "Sean, I'm so proud of you…" Mom, I hope I am making you proud with my accomplishments in my life. You have always said to me and others, "If you believe it and you pray on it, anything is possible." I Love you and Miss you…

My Mother-in-Law – *Kathy Waldron aka: Glamma*

After losing my mom right before my first son, Mason, was born, I was saddened that he wouldn't be able to meet his grandmother. Although my mom isn't here physically with us now, I know she is working through many of us each day, especially you. I tell Azure everyday how blessed I am to have you in my life and how wonderful you have been with Mason. It brings a smile to my face every time you are with him and as you give him that undivided attention that my mom would have given him if she were here. Kath, you are such a wonderful person and I am so blessed and proud to call you my mother-in-law. I Love You!

My Grandmother – *Aine Waldron aka: Mema*

As a gifted writer yourself, I am always so honored whenever you give my articles your two thumbs up! You are always the first one to read and like any of my stories that I post on social media and it always warms my heart and brings a huge smile to my face. You are the one that has encouraged me to actually write this book. I have put it on the back burner so many times and now I have finally taken your advice. Thank you for all of the constructive criticism and positive feedback on my writing throughout the years. You have motivated me tremendously to finally write this book! I Love you...

Before You Read...

The book you are about to read is a book about my personal life experiences and how they relate to business, more specifically the plumbing industry. My goal in writing this book is that I hope the reader can take away just one thing from my stories and apply what they have learned to their life and/or business. You DO NOT have to be a plumber to read this book! I am sharing a lot of my experiences as a father and as a plumbing professional with you. I hope you enjoy this book as much as I enjoyed writing it...

Table of Contents

My Story

There I was at the ripe age of 19, chasing my dreams of fame and fortune. I had a firm grip on the sticks, palms sweating and my mind was racing to remember the Intro, Bridge and Chorus of each song on the set list. I closed my eyes, took a deep breath and told myself to relax. "It's okay, Sean. Just keep breathing in through your nose for five seconds and out your mouth for three." It was something my mother had always told me to do when feeling overwhelmed or stressed. I picked up my head and looked out over my drum kit only to see a thick layer of smoke floating past the warm lights which shined down on the stage. "Wow, I'm really on stage about to play my first show in the Big Apple!" The Elbow Room was the name of bar and named appropriately so due to the long narrow room, which when filled with people, and it was, they were crammed like sardines standing elbow to elbow. They were all looking on to see what we were all about. Everything seemed to be moving in slow motion. I turned to the keyboard player to make sure he was ready, and then looked to the bass player. Both

1

acknowledged with a swig of beer, a nod and a cheers-like motion with the bottle. I smiled back, nodded and focused back on center stage. The bright stage lights felt as if they were two inches away from my forehead. The lead singer's dark silhouette approached the front of my kit. He nodded and said, "It's Showtime!"

The next four years were filled with 2-3 days a week of rehearsals, touring the North East a few times a month and long hours in the studio recording two albums. Not only was I committed full time to a band, but I was also in college from Monday to Thursday taking classes in the communication field. On Fridays and Saturdays, I was working with my father as an apprentice, getting my feet wet and trying to learn the trade. I was clearly juggling multiple things at one time and I wasn't quite sure which path my life was going to take. I had to make a decision on a career path soon, since I was now entering my junior year of college! I had a nice sit down with my mother and father and began to discuss my future with B.M.C. Plumbing and Heating. I was working extremely hard with the band and put in long hours each day of the week in order for my dream to come true. It was time to set a deadline on my music career. I gave myself a two-year window to strive for Rock Stardom. We got radio air play on some major stations and had the opportunity to open up for the premier of Jack Black's movie, "School of Rock," which was held at the Hard Rock Café in the heart of NYC. Although times were good with the band, my two-year window was up. Unfortunately, the music career did not take off as expected, but I wouldn't change the experience for the world! It was an unbelievable journey in which I learned and experienced a lot of new things and met a lot of wonderful people. It was time to face reality and make a decision to move forward with my career and life.

With my dreams of becoming a Rock Star behind me, I was off and running with my new goals and dreams ahead of me. I graduated college with a degree in communications and I was a full-time employee of B.M.C. Plumbing. I saw the potential in the family business and didn't mind getting dirty each and every day. After a few years had gone by and I had learned the trade, I was eventually in a truck of my own, handling service calls and starting to feel very confident about my plumbing abilities. After a long week of work one Saturday afternoon, a bunch of friends and I decided to head upstate for a relaxing weekend. There I was on the back deck with my feet up, full moon shinning, crickets singing, and enjoying a cold beer and a cigar. Things at this point just couldn't get any better! But they did! That night I had met my wife to be. I instantly fell in love. We began dating shortly thereafter and I knew this was the woman I would spend the rest of my life with. Before I knew it, I was riding in the car with her on our way up to meet her father. We arrived at her parents' house, my palms sweating and my heart beating a mile a minute. I was introduced to her father, Rich, and before I knew it, we were having a beer together talking about sports, music and sharing a few laughs together. "So, I hear you're a plumber, Sean." he said, "Yes." I replied, "I have been working with my father now for several years." That's all he needed to hear! Before I knew it, I was in the crawl space with a torch in my hand ready to solder together a copper line for an outside hose bib. I sparked up the torch and began to solder away! Right behind me was Rich looking on and probably praying that his house wouldn't go up in flames. Well, when you mix nerves, a flame and old insulation, you get an instant fire. I couldn't believe my eyes! The insulation had caught on fire but I tried to remain calm. "Rich, I need a bucket of water." (In a calm voice) "Sure Sean, I can just get you a wet rag instead if you need it to cool down your joints." "Yeah, that will work," I said. Just as he left the crawl space, I began to wail away with a rag to put out the orange glow in the bay. The words that were coming out of my mouth at that very moment were certainly not PG-13. Even with that small plumbing hiccup, he still allows me to do plumbing in his home and he still allowed me to take his daughter's hand in marriage...

Today, I stand in a damp cool basement with a wrench firmly gripped in my hands. I look around and see cobwebs and dust in the distance and I feel the heat beating down on my face from the clamp lights hanging from the beams. I look to my right at my co-workers and give them a nod, and then turn left to the boiler switch on the wall. "Are you guys ready? It's Showtime!" I flip that switch and the boiler fires.

Sean McCormack

I never thought that a sound like that would become music to my ears...

& Son

There I was waiting in anticipation for the greatest part of the day. I stared out the front window, like a dog waiting for the mailman. Curtains draped behind me and my nose glued to the cold window as my warm breath began to fog up the glass. "Where is he? Mom said he'd be here any minute," I'd keep saying to myself quietly. I could hardly wait any longer. Then I heard it. That truck engine getting closer and closer! There it was! I will never forget the color of that Dodge pickup truck. Seeing that bright cherry red color was the best part of the day! I screamed to my mom, "Mom! Mom! Daddy's home! Daddy's home!" I remember running like the wind. I couldn't turn the knob of the front door fast enough, knowing my dad would never go down the driveway hill without me. "Sean, slow down!" my mom said. It was too late for that; I was already in third gear! As I ran across the front yard towards my dad, I saw the front door of that truck open and my excitement grew even more. Reaching the truck with extreme excitement, I would clasp my hands on my dad, jumping to get into the truck with him as he gave me a boost up with his arms. Sitting on his lap with my hands locked on the steering wheel, nothing in the world could have made me happier! The unique smell of that truck, that plumbing smell we all know too well, will never escape me. We begin to roll slowly and make our decline down the hill, thinking I'm the greatest driver in the world. The truck comes to a stop at the bottom of the driveway and I think life just can't get any better than this! Little did I know, those weekday evenings riding with my father in his plumbing truck would turn into working with my father full time, and earning the right to have "& Son" proudly displayed on a truck of my own...

Back in those early childhood days, I looked up to my father like he was the greatest man in the world. The same still applies till this very day, as I look to follow is his footprints and one day take over the plumbing company. He has been extremely successful for over 30 years when he started with nothing and worked incredibly hard to build the business and raise a family. Thirty years ago, times were very different than they are now. Back then, business relied heavily on word of mouth to gain customers and putting small ads in church bulletins and the yellow pages. He created this company and treated it like his baby and still does to this very day. As times have changed, he has embraced them and has looked to me for incorporating new ways of building and growing this company...

Throughout the years of working with and for my father, I have grown tremendously; not only learning plumbing but also learning the business side as well. I learned how to treat customers, co-workers and others in the field. My father is not one to teach someone verbally, however, his actions spoke a thousand words. The biggest thing my father has done since the "& Son" has been added is that he is not stuck to his old ways. He has been open to new ideas that I present to him, such as advertising and incorporating a new look for the company. This is why he has been so successful throughout the years, because he knows how to adapt to the changing times. He could easily become stubborn and overprotective of his company since what he has established worked so well, why should he change? Because of his willingness to adapt, our business relationship has been great! This is a huge positive for any father and son company looking to make the transition from "mine" to "ours".

Just the other day as I was outside cleaning the truck back home, my two-year-old son came out to me and said, "Daddy, I want to help you. Daddy, I want to help you." I turned to him smiled and gave him a screw driver and said, "Go for it!" Away he went working on the truck as if it was the greatest thing in the world! I started to think, maybe one day I will have the opportunity of having my son jump on board the plumbing wagon and decide to work with me. Just as the thought crossed my mind, my son stopped what he was doing, looked at me, pointed to the truck and said, "Daddy, I want to drive! Daddy, I want to drive." And so we did...

Fatherly Advice

My father and I arrived at the job early that Tuesday morning, ready to dismantle an old, ancient beast of a boiler. We began to work hard for an hour or so before we decided to take a short coffee break. We sat down on the front stoop, sun shining brightly on our faces and a hot cup of coffee in hand. My father took a sip of his coffee, looked at me and said, "Sean, what we are doing in there right now, all of the plumbing, dismantling and installing of a boiler..." I replied, "Yes?." "Well, believe it or not, that's the easy part of this industry." I will never forget that day when my father told me that, and believe it or not, it's so true! Here are some other key factors my father shared with me that I believe are so important to apply every time you enter a customer's home...

Clean Up

Let's face it guys, we are not the cleanest tradesmen out there. We are surrounded with soot, dirt, grease and sludge every day. You

11

name it, we are in it! We could be working in a multimillion dollar McMansion or in a rundown hole in the wall home with cockroaches crawling throughout. No matter what the particular home looks like, I was always taught to make sure you leave the house cleaner than when you arrived. I will never forget this one job when we installed a hot water heater. All of the plumbing was immaculate! Nice clean solder joints, plumb gas line, perfect pitch in the flue pipe. It was something you would see in a commercial or magazine. We left that house like we were champs! Or so we thought! Later that day, my father gets that dreaded call. We accidentally stained a small portion of the client's carpet when taking the old heater out. Ugh, talk about coming down from a high!! I felt awful! All that hard, professional plumbing work and just that one small stain ruined everything! Ever since that day, I've become extremely cautious of not only making the plumbing clean and neat but also my surroundings in others' homes...

Trip to the Basement

I don't know about you, but there have been several times where I've been in a home to replace a fill valve and a flapper and out the door I go! I get to the truck, give my father a call, "Alright dad, we are all set over here!" My father replies, "Great! What kind of boiler and heater do they have down in the basement?" Let's just say that was the last time he ever asked that again! I learned my lesson real quick! Every house I enter now, I make sure I find a way down to that beautiful basement. My father has taught me through the years that just because a customer calls about one particular problem, it doesn't mean there isn't a future problem lurking elsewhere. So, instead of getting in and out of a home quickly, I now ask the customer if I could go downstairs to check the pressure of the main water coming into the house. This gets me downstairs where now I can take a look at other plumbing fixtures, hot water heaters and boilers. If something looks questionable, I will bring it to the customer's attention and possibly get a future job out of it! Oh yeah, don't forget to put those stickers on those heaters while you're down there!!

Dreaded Call Backs!

Let's face it; we've all had a couple of these pain in the butt calls! I don't know about you, but they are the worst! The one thing my father stresses to us more than anything is, NO CALL BACKS!! You can never be too overly cautious when working in the plumbing and heating industry. For example, in the early stages of my plumbing career, I was on a job changing out a kitchen sink faucet. I thought I nailed it. I left the house thinking I was a champ! WRONG! Yup! That dreaded call back! Got home that evening and got that phone call from my father. That sneaky packing nut on those angle stops was leaking. Ugh! The next day, I went back over there to fix the problem and I felt like such a failure. Now, learning from my mistakes, I know to check things more than once. I've learned to take my time on each job and ensure that everything is done properly and there are no loose ends! Taking your time on the job will definitely save you time and money in the long run.

These are only a few of many helpful tips my father has shared with me throughout the years. By applying these tips to my plumbing career, it has shaped me into a well-rounded contractor. Every day is a learning experience for me out in the field and I'm continuously looking to improve every chance I get. Hopefully by sharing a few tips my father shared with me helps you in your plumbing adventures!

Motherly Advice

It was a sunshine filled Friday morning as my bulldog (Norman) and I went out for a short walk. I had a sick feeling inside that something was just not right with my mother. She had been in and out of the hospital during the entire year fighting her battle with Leukemia at the young age of 52. She had spent several nights in the hospital and she was showing no signs of improvement. After Norman did his rounds, we headed back inside to find my wife on the phone with her eyes beginning to fill with water. I knew right away something had gone terribly wrong. I dropped the leash on the floor, hung my head, closed my eyes and began to cry. I couldn't believe my mother was gone. I then walked over to my wife and just needed to cry in her arms. The amount of water flowing from my eyes was similar to a relief valve opened full bore! No plumber was fixing this leak! But seriously, there was always one thing my mother taught me and each of her children. She always told us to give and help others and good things will come our way, and so, that's what I began to do in her honor...

Finding the Right One

Driving home one evening with my wife and son, I began to ponder which charity I would like to help. I started to think about my mom, as I did often, and all of the wonderful memories we shared together through the years. Just as the thought crossed my mind, the headlights from our car cast a bright glow on a large sign up ahead. The sign read, "Make – A – WISH Foundation, Hudson Valley, NY." Ah-ha! I began to nod my head in an up and down motion, "That's it," I whispered. I then tilted my rear view mirror to check on my son Mason and there he was happy as ever bouncing in his car seat with sugar flowing through his body because his aunts and uncles love to spoil him! I thought to myself, I am truly blessed to have a healthy, happy child. I cannot imagine what these children go through that are sick, let alone what the parents go through. I smiled back at him, readjusted my mirror, nodded again and thanked my mother for the sign. That very moment, I knew exactly what our company needed to do.

Help US, Help YOU, Help THEM

Help US, Help YOU, Help THEM was the slogan I had used while putting together our BMC Plumbing and Heating Charity Golf Classic. It was the perfect way for BMC Plumbing to reach out to our customers in support of this wonderful charity. I began to make brochures, flyers and coupons with special discounted offers for our customers on their particular plumbing and heating problems. By our customers **Helping Us**, by picking up the phone and calling us for our services, (**Help YOU**, the customer), they were contributing because we would take a percentage of each job accomplished and donate that money to the foundation/event (**Help THEM**). Our customers were so delighted to see that their plumbers were contributing to such a good cause! Each customer felt they were doing their part by using BMC Plumbing and Heating to help grant a child his or her wish. By incorporating a charity with your company, it not only looks great for your company, it also makes you feel great that what you accomplish each work day is contributing to a wonderful cause...

Your Turn!

We all know someone in our lives who has been troubled by life-threatening illnesses. For me, I wanted to reach out and help children because my mother always loved children. Also, becoming a father for the very first time, I couldn't imagine my child being sick and going through this tough time at such an early age. For you, you may have a special connection with some other charity. But, whatever that connection is for you and your company, don't be afraid to reach out and help others, because doing good things for others ALWAYS leads to good things in the end... (For photos from our Charity Golf Classic log onto: www.SEANthePLUMBER.com)

Getting to Know Your Customers

It was an early Saturday morning and I was responding to a call from a new customer. I spoke with the woman on the phone and she quickly described to me what the plumbing problem was, "My son couldn't get the shower to work so he began to play with the handle on the shower body and before we knew it, there was water everywhere! I have to run out for a bit to bring my son to the airport as he's going away to camp for a few weeks. The maid will be in the house and I will return shortly." Hmm, I said, "Okay, sounds good. I will be there soon." She gave me the address and I hopped into the truck and made my way over to the house. As I approached the neighborhood, the houses began to grow in size. "Wow, what a nice area." I said to myself. "These people must be living the good life around here. 262, wow! Nice house! 264, wow! Another nice house! 266, this is it!" I couldn't believe my eyes! It was larger than the other huge houses on the block. I turned into the driveway, which easily stretched the length of a football field, and eventually made my way to the front of the house. I immediately began to shake my head in amazement. I grabbed my tool bucket and drop light and headed to the front door. I knocked a few times and the maid opened the door and welcomed me into the house. "Come this way, the bathroom is all the way on the top floor." As I followed her around the house, I couldn't help but to look around in each room. There was an arcade room with games, a pool table and a ping pong table and across the hallway was huge movie theater with arena style seating, popcorn machine and a cotton candy machine! I thought these homes only existed in the movies! We eventually made our way to the bathroom where the woman showed me the plumbing problem. "This is it." As she pointed to the parts on the expensive marble top, she said, "Good Luck!" I chuckled and said, "Thanks!" After catching my breath from the mile walk to the bathroom, I began to dissect and reassemble the foreign shower parts. I was praying that the parts simply just got pulled off and needed to be tightened because the only way I was getting replacement parts for this shower was to call the manufacturer, which was probably some place overseas. I managed to conquer the task with only a few, "why the ****is this not fitting! These stupid expensive pieces of junk!" Let's be honest, we've all had these moments. If you say otherwise, you're simply lying! I had the water back on and the shower functioning properly in about 20 minutes.

After patting myself on the back for a job well done, I began to wrap up my tools and head back out to the truck to fill out the invoice. Just as the thought crossed my mind, the front door opened and a yell came from downstairs. "Sean! Are you upstairs!? I'm back from the airport. How are things going up there!?" She could have whispered and I still could have heard her voice from the echoes within the McMansion. "Everything is going well, Mrs. Green. Just wrapping up!" "Wonderful! I'm making some coffee. Would you like a cup?" I paused, "Sure!" I said. I had nothing lined up for the rest of the morning so why not. Plus this will give me a chance to find out what this lady is all about, how she got this home and hear some of her, I'm sure, very interesting stories. Before I knew it, I had a cup of coffee in my hands and I was standing in her beautiful living room looking out her giant windows which overlooked the Hudson

River. We began our small talk and started to discuss the effects hurricane Sandy had on her home, which sat only 50 feet from the shoreline. "Come with me down to the river and I will show you some of the damage. Bring your tools because I'll have you fix a leak underneath the outdoor kitchen sink." We made our way down the winding stairs which opened up to a beautiful outdoor seating area, bar, grill and kitchen. She showed me where the leak was coming from and I began to squeeze underneath the sink to fix the problem. "So, Mrs. Green, how long have you lived here? She replied, "About 6 years." "It's a gorgeous home, I must say." "Thank You, it's becoming too much for me though, I think I will be selling it shortly," she said. As she answered, I was cautiously looking around under the sink for any unusual creepy crawlers. "So, you have any kids?" I heard NO response! Oh no, I said to myself. I managed to wiggle out from the tight cabinetry and remove the cobwebs from my hair and mouth. I looked up at Mrs. Green as her head was hung low and tears began to fall from her face. She turned away embarrassed and looked out towards the river. "I had two sons...I lost my 16 year old about a year ago." She began to wipe her eyes and try to collect herself. I took a deep breath and shook my head, "I'm so sorry, I didn't know." We then began to share stories about life and I shared my tough times losing my mother at such an early age. We had a wonderful conversation for the next 10 minutes while I fixed the sink. I never thought that I would share something in common with Mrs. Green that Saturday morning. I will admit, I immediately judged her and chalked her up to be this wealthy, stuck up, I'm better than you, customer. Boy was I wrong! I learned a very valuable lesson that morning. Never assume what kind of customer you're going to meet and encounter. Yes, she owned a beautiful home and I never thought for a second I would meet this mystery wealthy woman. I thought I would accomplish the work at hand, leave an invoice and receive a phone call wondering why the job cost that much. However, when the job was finished, Mrs. Green personally handed me a check with a huge smile on her face. "Sean, it was wonderful meeting you. Your mother did a wonderful job in raising you. You made my day today. Thank you for listening to me." I never thought for a moment that this call would end with a comment like that, some tears and a giant hug.

As my father always told me and my co-workers, never judge any customer on their appearance or their home's appearance, regardless of whether they live in a McMansion or in a cockroach-invested hole in the wall. You should always give your all and apply your professional plumbing skills and good manners to each job. Always, respect the customer and clean up behind you. I learned a very valuable lesson that Saturday morning as I entered Mrs. Green's house, I never thought for a moment that the call would end the way that it did. I know for a fact the next time Mrs. Green needs plumbing work done in her home, she will not hesitate to pick up the phone and call us. Spending that little bit of extra time talking with her that morning and listening to her could only lead to good things and possible referrals from people she knows.

The Art of the Helper
Helping Hands" "

We've all been there; lying down in that dentist's chair with our mouth wide open hoping there are no cavities. I know, I know, you're thinking, "I thought this was a book about plumbing. Why are we talking about being at a dentist's office?" Well, while you lay there in that chair, we always notice that assistant who is handing the dentist all of his or her necessary tools to complete the task at hand. There is very little communication, if any, between the dentist and the assistant. The assistant knows exactly which instruments the dentist needs at all times no matter what the task is. This is a perfect example of how any assistant, in our case, a plumber's assistant/helper, plays such an important role out in the field.

The Basics

About 10 years ago, when I first started working on the weekends with my father, I didn't know what to expect and what my responsibilities were going to be on the job site. I knew I was there to help out and assist my fellow co-worker Glenn in any way possible when needed. The very first thing he had told me was, "Sean, I know a lot of this may seem overwhelming right now, but the most important thing to remember is to have a pencil in your ear and a tape on your waist. The rest will come with experience." He was right, my objective in the beginning stages was to measure and cut pipe and build a foundation for future responsibilities.

After learning the basics through the years, I began to learn more about the plumbing trade. I was not just cutting copper pieces according to what was shouted out to me. I began to learn the process of certain tasks at hand. The most important thing an apprentice can apply to their everyday tasks is the ability to know what the mechanic needs before they even ask for it. I found myself always thinking ahead of the mechanic. Not what does he need right now, but what will he need in the next minute or so. I always thought a couple of steps ahead of him. This made his ability to work a lot quicker and easier. When he is connecting his final fittings ready for soldering, I already had the torch fired up with solder in hand and a wet and dry rag ready to clean and cool the joints when finished. Another key point I was taught was to never just stand around with your hands in your pockets! There is hardly any time to stand around on the job. Trust me! I always occupied myself with something, either cleaning fittings, cleaning and organizing tools or simply ask questions. Even if you're not busy, either look like you're busy or make yourself busy! I found that these are two crucial components for any apprentice working in the field.

Through my years of being an apprentice, my co-workers would remind me to always feel free to ask ANY questions that came to mind. I took full advantage of those opportunities! The more I could learn the better. My brain was like a sponge taking in all the information possible. Still to this day, I am learning something new every week. There are so many things to learn in the Plumbing and Heating industry, so don't get stressed out! I would always find myself stressing and saying, "How am I going to learn all of this!?" So, if you're in this position currently, I advise you to relax and soak up as much

information as possible, take plenty of notes and
have some fun!

Dress to Impress

There I was, eating my lunch one afternoon, when out of the corner of my eye a plumber pulls up in his work van. The gentleman hops out of his truck and begins to head to the back of his vehicle to grab some of his tools. As I sit there eating my sandwich, observing the man, I began to shake my head in disappointment. The man looked as if he just rolled out of bed, threw on a shirt that was sitting in his hamper for weeks and jeans that were torn to shreds as if a lion got a hold of them! He proceeded to get his tools as I had the luxury of witnessing the "plumber's crack". It was that very afternoon I promised myself I would never leave my house looking like a "plumber".

Don't look like a "Plumber"

Before I leave each morning, I turn to my wife and jokingly ask her, "How do I look? I don't look like a plumber, right?" Relax, relax, I am only messing around here, but to a certain extent, it's true! Every plumber I know, including myself, has gone to work and when they arrive home they are a mess! Wood chips in your hair, down your pants and your shirt, ABS glue on your arms and elbows, dirt all over your hands and smelling like a plumber! However, leaving home in the morning looking like you just came home from work is a different story. Plumbers have always been associated with being slobs and showing off the famous "plumber's crack". I feel there are no excuses for any individual in any field of work, plumbers in our case, to leave their home looking like they just rolled out of bed. It's simply inexcusable and very unprofessional...

Steinbrenner Rules

George M. Steinbrenner was one of the most successful owners in all of sports to this very day. He was tough, loved to win and most of all believed in looking like a true professional. George was known for having all of his players looking clean cut and wearing their uniforms a certain way. He felt that looking professional while working every day says a lot about a person's character. This same principle Mr.

Steinbrenner enforced to his team should be enforced out in the field for us plumbers. I took Steinbrenner's Rules and applied them to myself as a plumber. For each day of the week, I have 5 clean pairs of pants and 5 clean shirts. I make sure I smell good and look good before I step out that door each morning. When Sunday evening arrives, I simply wash all of my clothes so that I am ready for a fresh start Monday morning! Not only does this make me feel great, but customers really appreciate having a clean professional entering their homes each day.

I am not by any means bashing us plumbers; however, I am encouraging all of us to start taking pride, not only with working with our hands, but in how we present ourselves each day when we wear our uniforms. Try it out! I guarantee you will look and feel like a million dollars and your customers will start to recognize and appreciate your professional appearance. So do yourself a favor and ask the question before heading out to work in the morning, "How do I look? I don't look like a plumber, right?"

Transforming Your Company

I have been working for the family business now for about 10 years. BMC Plumbing and Heating Inc. originated 30 years ago when my father Brendan McCormack branched off on his own and took flight, grabbing any plumbing and heating opportunity out there to make some money. Just graduating out of college, I had worked on and off with the company on the weekends before I became a full-time employee back in May 2005. While getting my feet wet learning the trade and absorbing as much plumbing knowledge as possible, I also learned how unorganized this company was. Don't get me wrong, my father has been very successful using his methods in running this company but things needed to be changed to bring this company to the next level.

Customer Organization

This is probably the most important aspect of running a successful plumbing business. "Sean, head over to Billy King's house over there on Smith Street. I'm not sure of the number of the house but it's blue with, I believe, yellow shutters or they could be grey." Ahhhhh! This needed to change instantly! We were not organized in our customer database so I took action! After the completion of every job, I took notes of the following and entered it into my customer database on my tablet: Name of customer, phone number, email, house address, the date of service, what we did and how much it cost, how they paid (credit card, cash, check), what kind of main water line they have coming into the house, do they have a gate valve or ball valve (crucial if you may need to shut down the main water. Those old gate valves sometimes don't close or won't open), how many gallons is the hot water heater, what condition is the boiler in, how many BTU's, so on and so forth...This helps tremendously! I can't stress how important this has been for our company. There have been many times where we showed up to a job trusting that the customer knew how many gallons the hot water heater was and they were wrong. The customers knew the gallons but did not know whether it was a high efficiency, standard or low boy heater. This makes a big difference when preparing for the job and ended up wasting precious time, especially when they were expecting 60 + people over in 2 hours for their party. So we had to return what we thought was a 50 gallon to replace with a high efficiency 50 gallon. Time = money! Knowing what you're faced with before arriving to the customer's home, whether it's having the right address or knowing what kind of heater they have, saves you time and money in the long run.

Follow Up

Follow-up calls are a MUST! I've found that at the end of a day, taking 10 minutes of your time to call up your accounts throughout the day is definitely worth it. I would find out how our services were and if there was anything we could do differently. You'd be surprised how pleased customers are with the follow-up call. It goes a long way.

Customer Email Address

When presenting the customer with an invoice of the work done, I always make it a habit of asking for their email address. I find this to be one of the more important pieces of information that needs to be taken; especially since email is the number one way of communication these days. Not only can people receive email through their computers, but now on their smart phones and tablets too. As soon as I finalize payment and get back in the truck, I immediately enter the customer (if not added already) to my customer database and the email list. BMC Plumbing and Heating has been doing this for a little over a year now and we've added over 200 + email addresses. The most important thing with email is NOT TO ABUSE it! I cannot stand getting emails from businesses every day. I don't see the need, plus any importance it may have wears off. Send an email once a month; include specials for the month or feature some new products out on the market. Again, don't abuse this because it will just negate its effectiveness.

Customer Rapport

Incorporating all of the above ideas into your company is essential; however, having a good rapport with your customer is most important. You can have an email list set up and do everything right plumbing wise, but without having the trust from the customer, there is no successful company. When entering a customer's house, I always pay attention to his or her name and shake their hand. I can't tell you how many times I have forgotten a customer's name! It's embarrassing. Knowing their name when asking them a question or to filling out the invoice helps with customer comfort. I always try to remember something specifically about each customer when I'm working there. For example, pet names, kid names, hobbies and important things a customer would share when talking with you. I always take these side notes down when entering them into the database to help refresh my memory when visiting again.

I've found that applying these key organizational skills to our company has helped tremendously and has saved a lot of time and money. I highly suggest incorporating these tools into your company and remember to have fun!

Ad-Trick-Tise

After a long day of work, I was on my way to meet a gentleman who worked at Provident Bank Park, which is the home of a local Can-Am baseball team in New York. I was looking to discuss some possible advertising opportunities with him within the stadium confines. I arrived at the stadium and was greeted by Mr. Goldstein and was given a quick tour of the area. During our stroll, he began to point out possible options for advertising. As he was speaking, all I could think of was, "How much is this going to cost..." After our walk, we sat down and I showed him some of my ideas for my "Triple Play Boiler deals." Basically, if you have BMC Plumbing install a boiler, you will receive 10 percent off the installation, four tickets, and lunch vouchers to the game. A portion of proceeds would be donated to the Make-A-Wish Foundation. He loved my ideas and we began to negotiate the different pricing options. So, I began to point at the different advertisements in the stadium. "How much is that huge billboard in center field?" The price made my jaw drop to the ground! I couldn't believe it! I then said, "David, that is way out of our price range. What other options do you have?" He began to tell me more and he was able to get the price down to what I thought was somewhat reasonable. David knew I was still in shock about what they were asking. He put his hand on my shoulder and said, "Sean, have you ever looked into having a major company sponsor you and your business?" I looked at him with confusion, but was very interested in what he had to say. "No, what do you mean?" I asked. "Sean, you get a company to advertise with you and they put up half the cost. If they believe in your company, what you're advertising, where you're advertising and the price is right, there is no reason why that company wouldn't sponsor you and BMC Plumbing." Now that I have a rough idea of what David and the organization are asking for in advertising space, I can begin my brainstorming ideas of what company would be willing to sponsor BMC Plumbing and Heating. I didn't just want to reach out to just any company, however, I wanted a company that I trusted and that believed in the products they sold. All plumbing, heating and HVAC companies have certain brands and products they are loyal to and prefer over other brands. For BMC Plumbing, it was a no brainer! ECR International / Dunkirk was the one company we trusted when using their products, specifically Dunkirk Boilers, which we have been using for many years. I jumped onto the computer and started to research how I could contact someone from the company. This is where social media helped tremendously. Between Facebook and LinkedIn, I was able to connect with some of the individuals over at ECR International. I came up with a business plan, which included: Cost of advertisement, location of advertisement opportunity and duration of ad, etc. Shortly thereafter, I received a positive phone call back from Dunkirk to say they loved my ideas. We then began our negotiations and ideas for a sign at the stadium. Since the deal was split 50/50 in cost, we ensured that both parties had equal opportunity to advertise their product on the banner. Not only did we have a large banner displayed in the stadium, but we were able to set up a tent and table for a few of the games to display some of Dunkirk's newer products and help advertise BMC Plumbing.

This was a huge success for both companies and the beginning of a great business relationship! Something you may NOT know...

After reading a bit about sponsorships in business, I began to find out some interesting information that I was not aware of. Almost every plumbing supplier that we go to every day has money which is set aside for advertising/promotional purposes. This money is referred to as co-op money. What is co-op money? Many suppliers, manufactures and distributors offer cooperative advertising programs (co-op for short) that your business can use. The term cooperative, in a business advertising context, means just what it says. If you (your plumbing company) spend some money, the manufacturer will also spend some money f to cooperate to get the advertising opportunity up and running and sell the manufacturer's product. The most important thing to do is ask! Talk to your marketing and/or advertising managers of your supply house. These supply houses are not going to just offer this money to you! If you are a loyal customer to the supply house and to a specific company product and have a good advertisement plan/idea, there should be no reason why the supply house wouldn't agree to work with you. I learned a lot that evening when I took a walk around Provident Bank Park with Mr. Goldstein.

There are always ways to cut some costs when advertising your business, which can also lead to developing some new and wonderful business relationships with other people. My relationship with Dunkirk is great. They saw an opportunity in me and our company and were willing to give us and our ideas a shot. So, the next time you look to do some advertising for your plumbing company, don't be afraid to reach out and ask!

Man's Best Friend

As I lay in the most comfortable bed in the world, I slowly opened up my eyes, stretched, turned to my left and saw my wife lying beside me. She gave me a huge smile and said, "Wow! What a party!" I was greeted with a kiss and a huge hug from her as she whispered into my ear, "I can't believe we are actually married." I replied, "I know it's crazy! The day flew by so fast." After only getting a few hours of sleep the night before, I really needed some rest. So I rolled back over and sunk my body into the pillow-top mattress. I could have lain there all day! Unfortunately, that didn't happen because nature was calling! As I peeled the four or five layers of sheets and blankets off me and swung my legs towards the side of the bed, all I saw were hundreds of colored, ripped opened envelopes on the hotel bedroom floor. I began to laugh at the mess in front of me. It looked as if a lion came in and went to town! "We made out pretty well, huh?" I said to my wife, as I rubbed my head that was hurting from too much partying the night before. "Yeah, everyone who attended gave really nice gifts," she said. My wife began to rattle off the amount we ended up with. It was music to my ears. I sat up at the edge of the bed and slowly turned to her, smirked and said, "You know what that means, right?" My wife looked at me with her left eyebrow raised and that confused, scared look on her face. "No. No. No. I am not getting a bulldog right away. I want to enjoy this time we have together, just you and I. No dog yet," she said. A week had passed and there we were driving in the car to Catawissa, PA to pick up our puppy! I had one hand on the steering wheel and the other holding my wife's hand, as I continued to convince her why this was such a great idea. A few hours later, we pulled up to the house and saw two small bulldog puppies out in the yard. The woman let both of the pups out of the enclosed fence and one pup ran the other way and the other (the smart one) came right up to my wife and sat his wrinkled butt right on her lap. He then looked up at her with that sad puppy face and I knew right away we were adding another member to our little family. A year passed and our bulldog, Norman, was making himself right at home. We shared so much laughter because of him and still do to this day. We treated Norman as if he was a child of ours, and I know there are many of us out there who do the same with their pets. We brought Norman with us everywhere we went, and he even had his own car seat in the back. I know, it's bad. Every time we went out and took our walks with Norman, we couldn't move five feet without being stopped by people asking to pet him. "What's his name?" "How old is he?" "Does he drool a lot?" "Does he snore?" "How much does he weigh?" "Does he suffer from allergies?" We got stopped so much that I had all the answers down pat. I now know exactly how a celebrity feels when they are constantly being stopped and asked the same questions over and over! There were times when he would draw such crowds of people at once, I couldn't believe my eyes. During one of those times, a gentlemen standing to my left jokingly said, "Hey, you should charge people for petting your dog. You would make a lot of money!" And there it was again, that ever so famous light bulb right above my head...

In the past when I attended the street fairs in my town, I found it very difficult to get people over to my tent and interested in BMC Plumbing. This is where my best friend Norman comes into play. I had an idea and I needed to put the plan into effect at the next street fair. I got shirts made up for the event that said "TEAM BMC" on each of them. I got one for myself, my wife, my son and, of course, Norman. We eventually made it to our designated area, after, of course, being stopped many times with Norman, and began to set up shop. I'm not exaggerating when I say this but our tent was mobbed with people just wanting to see and pet Norm. This is where my strategy paid off! Every person who asked to pet Norman had to donate $1 towards the Make-A-Wish Foundation. With each donation, my wife handed them a brochure and a business card as well as had them sign our mailing list. People were more than willing to help out a good cause and, on top of that, they became very interested in our company. People were glad to see a local company supporting a great charity and they got to talk about their own pets and share some of their own stories with us. It was a homerun! We were able to raise close to $300 for the charity, and we gained some new customers while doing so. Now, wherever Norman and I go, I make sure I have business cards right in my back pocket to hand out!

The moral of the story here, guys, is to be creative with your company. The first couple of times I attended these street fairs, I wasn't getting many people to our tent. No one was interested in a plumbing company. You have to add spice, excitement and creativity in order to attract people to your business. Whether that's a pet, charity, raffles or giveaways, you should find something that works and start growing your business!

Not much has changed since we made the decision to bring Norman into our family. I still sleep in a very comfortable bed, however, when I turn to my left, I no longer see my wife first. Between her and I, there lays a drooling, snoring bulldog named Norman, and I wouldn't change it for the world. Be creative and have fun promoting your business!

The Puddle

It was 3:00a.m. My dog, Norman, shot me a look and began to whine and continued to look out into the bedroom hallway.

"Lay down Norm, Mama will be right back. She's just using the bathroom," I said.

I flipped my pillow over to the cool side to lay back down and try to get some more sleep before it was time to rise. Before I knew it, I shot another look at the clock and it was 3:15a.m. I turned over to see if my wife, Azure, was back in bed, but she wasn't. I then looked toward Norman and he was still sitting there looking at the bathroom light which glowed underneath the door onto the floor. It was very abnormal for my wife to be in the bathroom for 15 minutes. She's usually in and out in less than 2 minutes, tops!

"Something isn't right here," I said.

I hopped out of bed and walked briskly to the bathroom door.

"Azure, are you okay?" I asked.

"I'm in a lot of pain, Sean. My stomach is killing me," she replied.

"h, no. It was time! But it couldn't be! On the actual due date!? I thought to myself.

"Did you call the doctor?" I asked.

"Yes, she said to wait until the morning and see how I feel. I'll be right out," she said.

This gave me some kind of relief and I made my way back into the bedroom to calm Norman down. Two minutes later, Azure came back into bed and tried to rest. I began to watch the clock and kept tabs on the time in between each shooting pain she reported. First, it was every four minutes, then every three minutes.

"Azure, I think we need to head to the hospital. You could be ready to give birth," I said.

"OK, OK, let me call the doctor again," she said.

Just as she stood up, I heard water hitting the wood floor.

"What was that?" I asked.

"My waters broke!" she replied.

I jumped out of bed, as did Norman, to see what was going on. I quickly threw a towel on the puddle before Norman got his nose into it! I plopped Norm back onto the bed, began to throw our clothes into a duffle bag, and headed off to the hospital! Twelve hours later, Mason Richard McCormack was born at 6 pounds and 9 ounces.

After two days at the hospital, things started to die down a bit and it was time to take the munchkin home. We carefully placed him into his car seat and bundled him up as if we were heading outside into a blizzard. Mind you, it was July! We made our way to the car and I placed Mason's carrier into the base of the car seat. Click.

"Is he secure, Azure?" I asked.

"I believe so," she said.

"I think I heard a click," I said.

Not believing myself, I began to lift up on the handle of the carrier to ensure the seat was secure.

"OK, I believe it's good," I said.

Azure then jumped into the back seat next to Mason and I nervously took the wheel in my hands. We were on the road and I was on high alert! My eyes were scanning the road constantly and I was nervously looking in each of my mirrors. I stayed in the far right lane of the highway, cruising at a speed of 30 miles an hour. I was being so overly cautious and aware of my surroundings the entire trip.

I kept checking my blind spots, using the turn signal way in advance before switching lanes and keeping a more than safe distance from the car in front of me. What was only a 20-minute drive on a normal day took us close to an hour. But, we managed to arrive home safe and sound. At the time, I thought I was being too overly cautious with my driving skills. However, it was so crucial for me to triple check every decision before making a move with such an important package to be delivered. You can never be too cautious!

It was a Friday afternoon and my co-worker Glenn and I arrived at a house to install a 75-gallon hot water heater. Glenn headed to the basement to begin the dismantling phase, and I headed upstairs to open up a few faucets to help drain the heater. Things started out smoothly and then the ever so famous Friday-late-afternoon-curve-balls started to come our way! You name it, it happened.

The cold feed gate valve to the heater wasn't holding, so we needed to shut off the main water supply to the house. Yep, you guessed it. The valve now at the meter wasn't holding and it was time to call the water company. We all know that waiting for the water company to arrive isn't the fastest process in the world. But, eventually they showed up and I was able to sweat a ball valve on in no time.

After several hours on the job, it was time to fill up the 75-gallon beast. Glenn began to feed the heater with water and I made my way upstairs to ensure all fixtures were turned off. While upstairs, a call came in on my cell from a customer and my focus was directed to the phone call. Once the tank was filled and all of the air was out, I shut the hot side of the kitchen faucet and made my way back to the basement.

Glenn and I began to quickly clean up because it was getting late and we wanted the weekend to begin! All of the tools were quickly wrapped up and put into the truck. I then made my final go-around to ensure there were no leaks or tools left behind. While in the basement, I heard water running. I quickly went to the meter to see if the needle was spinning, and it was!

"Oh, no!" I said.

I ran like the wind! I raced up those basement stairs and began my frantic search for a running faucet. My mind was racing and counting all of the fixtures I had opened.

"Kitchen sink, bathroom sink, shower…. The tub!!!" I finally recalled.

I quickly sprinted upstairs to the second level and burst through the master bathroom door. There it was. The tub on legs was filled to the brim! The homeowners had left the plug in the drain. I quickly shut the valves, and took a step back with my eyes wide and in total shock.

"Oh my god, that was close," I said.

All I could think about was what if we had left that house with the tub running. The homeowners were away for the weekend and the place would have been flooded! I knelt down near the tub, shook my head, and carefully reached into the tub and pulled the plug.

The situation on that Friday afternoon could have turned really ugly. We all have been in these situations as plumbers, and they can be very scary! I learned a very valuable lesson that afternoon, you can never be too cautious while plumbing. My mind was elsewhere when I was talking on the phone and I was not focusing on the job at hand. If I took my time and triple checked everything, this possible near disaster would have been avoided.

Whether you're sweating pipe in a tight spot, dealing with gas and water, or taking that nerve racking ride home from the hospital with your baby, you can never be too cautious! Trying to throw a towel on this possible "puddle" wouldn't have cut it.

Detective Plumb

All of the trick-or-treating was completed and we had ourselves one happy, hyper, little Spiderman, who was ready to knock on at least another hundred houses, if we let him. Mason's plastic pumpkin was filled to the brim with every type of sugary candy one could imagine. We loaded into the car and all I could think about was sinking my teeth into a nice burger. "OK, any superheroes who want to go out to dinner!?" I yelled. "Spiderman?" I got a smile and a nod yes, because he was too busy scarfing another piece of candy into his mouth. I looked to my wife and said, "Mrs. Captain America, I hope you're hungry because HULK-IS-HUNGRY!" Yes, I was all dressed up as the great green giant HULK. I was in green from head to toe and sporting steroid-sized green foam HULK hands. We headed into town and began to circle the parking facility, looking for a spot that was somewhat close to the restaurant because the sky had just opened up and it was pouring rain. "Right over there, Sean. That truck is about to leave," my wife said. Just as we pulled up to the spot, the gentlemen driving the truck stepped on

56

the gas and cut the wheel a bit early, slamming into the vehicle right next to him. "Oh my god! Someone get his license plate info," I said. But, no such luck as the truck speed off with visibility at a minimum due to the fog and rain. We quickly called the police and we were told to stay put until an officer had arrived on the scene. About five minutes passed and a patrol car rolled up to the damaged vehicle. We got out of the car and the officer began his investigation of the accident. "What was the gender of the driver? What color was the vehicle? What side of his truck was hit? What was the make and model of the truck? License plate info? Which direction did he go? You name it, he asked it. We tried our best to give the most accurate answers because it was very difficult to see due to the inclement weather. While the officer was jotting down all of the info we were supplying him, I began to think about my career as a plumber and how the officer and I shared some similar detective work in common. In my earlier years as a plumbing apprentice, I wasn't the best detective for the job. But honestly, who is when they first start out, right? I had my fair share of detective blunders, but, most importantly, I learned from my mistakes. When I used to enter a home or apartment, I didn't take the time to ask the customer many questions, and I just went right to work. For instance, there was a time I arrived at a home and all I did was listen to the customer go on and on about how every time someone flushed the upstairs toilet, the seal would leak and the floor would get wet. "I know for sure, whenever I flush this toilet, the tile floor will get wet. I believe the wax gasket needs to be replaced," the customer told me.

This is where I made my biggest mistake as a plumbing detective. Without asking any further questions or even investigating the plumbing scene, I just went to work, pulled the toilet and replaced the wax seal. Job well done, right? Wrong. An hour later, we received a call from the customer saying the toilet was still leaking and that the seal must have been defective. I shot back over to the house and I began to observe the situation a bit closer. When I flushed the toilet, I found that the tank to bowl seal was shot and there was the slightest stream of water that followed the curve on the bowl and ended up building at the base of the toilet. "You son-of-gun!" I whispered. After explaining the evidence to the customer, I got to work and made the proper repair. Small potatoes! If I had just taken my time and not only listen to the customer, but perhaps ask a few questions and investigate the scene a bit more, I could have avoided the call-back, and the job would have been completed the first time. This has happened to me before with those tricky "shower leak" calls, where the customer and I both think it's a plumbing related leak, and before we know it, the sheetrock ceiling is cut open and there is no sign of a leak on any plumbing joint. It just ended up being cracks and seams in the tile or where the tub meets the floor. Again, lesson learned there, and that will never happen again! So, now with a lot more years under my belt in this plumbing world, I've learned a whole lot when it comes to investigating the plumbing scene before diving right in. Whenever I enter a home or apartment, I always make sure not only to listen to the customer but to also ask a bunch of questions. By doing so, I am now able to really focus in on the real plumbing issue and make the proper repairs the first time. By taking those five to ten extra minutes, I definitely save a lot of time in the long run. If the police officer that evening didn't use proper protocol and didn't ask the important questions, he would have just tried to chase down the vehicle that fled the scene 10 minutes prior to his arrival. Most likely, he would have just wasted his time meandering around the town trying to hunt down a man who was long gone. Instead, he took his time to investigate the damage to the other vehicle, got all of the info he needed, and a week later, ended up finding the gentlemen with that very same truck getting repaired at a local auto body shop. The most important thing when entering a home is to not panic and react right away to the situation at hand. Take your time, listen to the customer, investigate the possible problem, and ask plenty of questions. Over and out.

Dr. Plumber

I could easily run past my mom, grab and turn the handle, run down that hallway, out that door and escape! I'd be free! I thought to myself. Then reality set in. IF I got past my mother and managed to get that door opened and make it to the parking lot, who would drive me home? I was doomed and there was no way out. Those fluorescent lights were brighter than ever, those cotton balls in the glass tubes made my stomach turn and that biohazard symbol on that container that hung on the wall scared me to death. I sat there nervously looking at all of the above and fixated on the diagram hanging on the wall of the human body. I heard the faint voices just beyond the door as they grew closer and closer. Here they come, here they come, I said to myself. "Mom, are you sure I don't need a shot?" I asked. "Yes Sean..." my mom said. Just as she answered, the door knob turned and now there was no escape. The lady entered the room all bubbly and holding that folder that would decide whether or not I get out of here alive! "Why, hello Sean, how are we doing today?" the doctor asked, I didn't answer. "He's

OK, just a little nervous," my mom replied. "Oh, there is no need to be nervous Sean," the doctor said, as she sat down next to me on the crinkly paper. She continued to check my heart, throat, ears, temperature and pressure. "OK, looking good," the doctor said. YES! I am home free! I thought to myself. Then she took another look at that folder. "Hmm, it seems that Sean is not up to date with his…" she continued to rattle off some obscure name, aka: SHOT!

Long story short, they needed six nurses to peel me off and grab me from out underneath the chairs that were in the room. I kicked, screamed and threw punches in the air. I could taste the snot from my nose and salt from my tears. And, the last thing I remembered was that smell of rubbing alcohol. Although I'd like to say that things have changed since those early childhood days when dealing with doctors, unfortunately they haven't. However, I do take on the same responsibilities as a nurse or doctor would with a patient when dealing with plumbing and heating.

There are a lot of similarities when it comes to the human body and plumbing. I look at a house before I enter, and think as if the house is a patient. The house has copper pipes like veins, pumps like the human heart, check valves used the same way as the ones found on the arteries, pressure and temperature and, not to mention, the waste lines. What comes in must come out! I'll give you an example of how I use the comparison of the human body and plumbing when it comes to dealing with homeowners. Whenever I enter a house, before I leave, I always check the water pressure with my gauge. If the pressure is through the roof, I notify the owner and make them aware of the issue at hand. I begin to explain to them that if the pressure in the house exceeds a certain psi, they must consider changing the 25AUB regulator at the main water supply entering the house. This is where I get that look as if I'm trying to run up the bill on them. I always bring the home owner to the gauge and show them the current pressure of the house. I then begin to explain to them how the water pressure is similar to blood pressure in the human body. "If you go to the doctor and he or she checks your blood pressure and it is on the high side, your doctor will probably make you aware of the situation and explain to you that having high blood pressure is not good for you or your organs," I explain. "It puts too much stress and strain on your most vital organs in your body, i.e. (heart, kidneys, etc.), the same applies with your house." I go on to explain, "If you have high water pressure, it will begin to put major strain on your water lines and all of your fixtures in the house, which could cause fixtures to leak and become damaged." I simply associate the human body to the plumbing in their home so they can better understand. And nine times out of ten, they give me a look, nod and the go ahead for changing out that faulty regulator. I NEVER thought that I'd share any similarities with that "evil" woman who carried the "evil" yellow folder! But I do!

After every boiler we install or service, I keep records of what was done on the boiler with a date, parts installed, and any questionable things about the system. So, in the future when I return to service the boiler, I simply grab the yellow folder that hangs on the wall next to the boiler and see what work was done in the past. This gives me a good indication of what may need to be changed on my "patient." You should try it! If we install a new boiler, I make up a sheet with the "date of birth" and continue to keep records from there on out. If it's an old boiler that we service, I simply keep records of things that were done or certain things to keep an eye out for. This gives the technician who arrives at the job a good indication of what is at hand. The only thing that is different between a plumber and a doctor in this case is that the "patient" can't kick, scream or try to run away!

Hibachi Bucket

There I was, sitting in one of my favorite places to eat. It was a big night out because it was my birthday. But, not just any birthday, it was the BIG 3-0! I sat there with all of my family, friends and loved ones with my favorite drink in hand: The Zombie! If you haven't tried this drink, you must be careful because it's very strong. As I'm sitting there enjoying my cocktail, eating my favorite salad covered in ginger dressing, and slurping down the wonderful taste of Miso soup, I see the tall white hat appear from the back of the restaurant. "Here he comes!" I said. I turned to my wife and said, "This never gets old." I sit at the edge of my seat with my neck extended out like a turtle. "Yup, that's our guy. He's coming this way," I said. He was pushing his cart, which was filled with tons of fresh lobster, steak, rice, shrimp, chicken and veggies. He pulled his push cart right beside our Hibachi table and greeted us with a smile. He went around the table and made sure everyone's order was correct. As he was doing so, I couldn't help but notice the cart filled with food, sauces and gadgets. Also, his belt held several knives and tools. He began to clean the cooking surface and the show began! He was like a ninja up there. He was grabbing the food off the cart, throwing it on the grill, and he was flipping his tools in the air and making the ever so famous volcano! I watched the chef do his thing, grabbing the tools and food without even glancing at the cart or his belt. I was amazed. I began to observe him and his technique. He had a system with that cart and his tools. He could have prepared that meal with his eyes closed! Not only was I entertained by his performance, but I was so impressed with his organization of his push cart and belt. As the warm volcano flame lit up my face and got applause from the table, I nodded and the light bulb above my head went on!

That following Monday, I knew I had to start organizing my tool bucket right away. I made a trip to the local supply house and purchased a few bucket buddies for my spackle bucket. Things needed to change instantly. No more throwing tools into a bucket and taking 20 minutes trying to find one tool that I need for the job at hand. I dumped all of my tools on the pavement and began to separate all of the hand tools from the soldering tools. I installed the bucket buddies on two separate buckets and began to put my hand tools in one bucket and the soldering tools in another. There were so many different pockets throughout the bucket buddy I wasn't sure if I'd fill each one up. But of course I did! I designated a pocket for each tool. I kept the channel locks in the two outside pockets next to each other with a Teflon tape in front of each channel lock. I made sure I was so precise with where I put each tool so I was aware where each tool was. If I or my helper needed the Teflon tape, I knew exactly where it was - the pocket right in front of the channel locks! I did this all throughout the tool bucket. Next to the channel locks was the snips and next to them was the crimp tool and the inside pouch was lined with five or six different screw drivers and nut drivers. I did the same with my second bucket which was designated for all of my soldering material. Each tool had a certain place from the striker to mini cutters to solder to cleaning brushes and flux. I know, I know. You're thinking, "Sean you are a lunatic!" I'm not though. You must apply this method to your tool buckets because it will save you time, money and aggravation. Not only will it save you time finding the right tool, it will also save your helper from wanting to pull out his hair! If I'm underneath a sink and I ask my helper for a certain tool, he simply reaches down to the tool bucket and knows exactly where the tools are. I LOVE IT! Not only did I change and organize my tool buckets, but I made all of my co-workers do the same. No more messy tool buckets allowed in BMC Plumbing and Heating.

I made the workers organize their buckets exactly how mine was organized. This helped tremendously because no matter what helper was with which technician, the tool buckets were identical. Time = Money! I know you never thought I'd make the correlation between a plumber and a Hibachi chef, but I did! My tool buckets may not hold fresh lobster, steak, rice, shrimp, chicken and veggies, but I know that making this change with my tools will only help me become more organized and save more time on each job. Plumbers may not be able to amaze a customer with a volcano made of onions but you do get the occasional customer who is very impressed with your organized tool bucket. Seriously though, apply this technique to your company and I guarantee it will make you and your helpers much happier. Oh, and again, be careful with those Zombie drinks.

I Do.

My alarm sounded early that Saturday morning and I slowly opened my eyes. The sun was peeking through my window, and I could smell the fresh cut grass from my neighbor's yard. At first I thought I had just another work day ahead of me and then I sat up in my bed and remembered today was the big day! A smile came across my face and I jumped out of bed. Before I knew it, the nerves began to set in and the big day was on its way. I scarfed down a big breakfast, took my shower and jumped into my tuxedo. Before I knew it, I was outside the house posing for what seemed like a thousand pictures. My groomsmen and I were then directed into our limousine and went on our way to the church. We arrived, took another thousand pictures, and before I knew it, I was standing at the altar, palms sweating, anticipating the arrival of my wife-to-be. The church was filled with friends and family all dressed to impress. A cameraman stood to my left with his monster lens staring straight at me, ready to catch my first reaction upon seeing my wife. "All right, Sean, you'll be OK," I told myself under my

71

breath. "Everything is going to go smoothly and then we're off to the big party. Just keep your emotions in check and hold it together." Now, everyone who knows me also knows that I am a very emotional person. I knew it would be nearly impossible for me to hold back those tears, but I kept telling myself I wasn't going to cry. The music began, and everyone in the church stood up and faced the back of the room with their phones and cameras ready to snap away. You're going to be fine, Sean. Don't faint. Don't cry. Keep it together. I kept telling myself this over and over, repeatedly. I raised my head and there she was, with her father walking down the aisle. Then the water works began. Tears streamed down my face and the cameraman was right there to capture every one of them! The Mass went on, and then it was time for the vows. We promised we would be loyal to one another and love one another, "til death do us part."

I know you are probably thinking right now, "Sean, why are you telling us about your wedding day?" Well, loyalty, trust and love are three major components of any marriage. They are also key factors in our field of work when it comes to the products and companies we buy from and use day in and day out. I am going to share with you a company that I am loyal to and trust, Dunkirk/ECR International. There is no better feeling in my industry than seeing that wood crate sitting in the driveway when I arrive at the job. That nice blue colored beast of a boiler ready to be released from its cage! Of course, I'm talking about those Dunkirk Boilers! BMC Plumbing and Heating Inc. have been installing Dunkirk boilers for many, many years now. I remember when I first began working with my father as an apprentice. He would often tell me and our workers how much he loved those Dunkirk boilers. Back then I didn't know much about them, but I did love that beautiful blue jacket that surrounded those cast iron sections! As the years went on and I began to understand and learn more about boilers, I realized why my father loved and appreciated the Dunkirk products. Dunkirk/ECR always seemed to keep the installer in mind when designing these wonderful units. Through the years, we've installed quite a few of these blue beasts, including their WPSB Series, PSB Steam Boiler Series, XEB Series and even the wall-hung high efficiency DKVLT, aka The HELIX VLT! If you haven't got your hands on this beautiful piece of art yet, I highly recommend looking into it. I also got to know some of the team members from ECR International, such as Bob Shea (regional manager), David Walsh (director of sales) and Carolyn Kuczynski (independent marketing consultant). BMC Plumbing and Heating has had the opportunity to work with the above people from ECR to create some advertising opportunities locally. They were more than willing to listen to my ideas, and we were able to create a wonderful relationship that stands to this day. As I said, trust, loyalty and love are three elements that sustain any relationship. In our case, as contractors, I feel it's crucial to work with a company that we trust, and a product that we love to install. I am a loyal customer and installer of all Dunkirk/ECR products, and I encourage you to learn about their boilers. Maybe you'll have the chance to install a few down the road. There is no better feeling in the industry than sitting down with my co-workers and sipping coffee next to that beautiful blue boiler after a hard day's work. The sound of that gas valve opening and that main burner firing! It's true love, 'til death do us part.

Dancing on Your Own

It was a typical Monday evening when I arrived home from a long day of work. I was greeted at the front door by my son Mason and our English bulldog, Norman. Mason ran into my arms screaming, "Da-da's home! Da-da's home!" Norman barked loudly and drooled all over my work pants, while he was looking for his much needed TLC as well! "How was everyone's day?" I asked, looking in my wife's direction. "We all had a great day, but Mama needs a vacation," she replied. I smiled and gave my wife a kiss hello. After catching up on the day, I hit the shower and got into my pajamas. For the next hour, Mason and I became every superhero or Ninja Turtle you could imagine—leaping over toys on the floor, diving onto all the beds and couches in the house, and getting chased by evil villains! After we managed to thwart all the crime in the house, it was time for dinner, bath, teeth brushing and bed where we began our nightly storytelling routine. After Mason fell asleep, I made my way back into the living room where I found my wife curled up on the couch. Her eyes were glued to the T.V. I asked myself, "What could she be watching so intensely?" Just as the thought crossed my mind, my question was answered. "Ladies and gentlemen, 'Dancing with the Stars'!" the voice on the T.V. roared. Ah-ha! I said to myself. I should have known. It was Monday night, which is "Dancing with the Stars" night. I mean that in a good way. I retreated into the kitchen, grabbed myself a cold beer, sat down next to my wife and began to watch along with her. That's right, guys, I admit it! I occasionally watch Dancing with the Stars with my wife. As I watched with her that Monday night, I was blown away by, not only, the extremely extra talented dancers, but also how creative the dancers were every week. I couldn't believe it. Each week we watched, the dancers had to come up with a new routine that required a lot of creativity. OK.

So, now you know one of my guilty pleasures, and you are probably wondering where I'm going with this one. Well, as you all know, in our industry there are many ways in which we can utilize the ability to be creative. With all of the tools and materials we use day in and day out and all of the different circumstances we encounter each day, we are faced with using that intelligent muscle between our ears. I can't tell you how many times my co-workers and I had to be creative when lugging a beast of a boiler down some old rickety stairs. The things we have to do to get a boiler or heater safely up, down, in, or out it becomes comical at times. A boiler job, as we all know, is a team effort and is not something one man can handle on his own. However, when it comes to those situations where you are on a job with just you and yourself and need that extra pair of hands, sometimes you have to get a lot more creative than normal. Whenever I'm faced with installing a kitchen sink faucet on my own, I'm usually putting my creativity to good use. Every time I got the faucet in place and I got myself situated under the sink to install it, the faucet would just keep tipping forward. Having only two hands at my disposal, I needed to put my brain to work and ended up finding some creative uses for a few everyday items in my handy-dandy tool bucket (Liquid wrench, putty, and some Teflon tape). I know it sounds funny, but I tell ya', it certainly did the trick! It's amazing how we all sometimes need to put our creative minds to work; whether it's being creative with my son's bedtime stories, when I'm at work underneath a sink, or when I'm coming up with an idea for my next chapter to write (like this one). Next time when you're out in the field and you don't have your "dance" partner with you on the job, use that magnificent thing between your ears and make it happen! I know I'm not the only one out there with creative ideas. Please send me some of your masterpieces! Find me on twitter @seantheplumber1 or email me, seanmccormack99@yahoo.com. Have fun out there, people, and be creative!

Hole-In-One

It was a beautiful Sunday afternoon with the sun shining bright, birds chirping and a nice breeze in the air. Nothing mattered more in the world, at such an early age of 15, than playing golf with my brother. Rich and I just finished up the seventh hole, each coming away with a lousy double bogey. "Ugh, what an awful hole for us!" I said to Rich. "I know that hole is never easy, but there is still plenty of golf to play," he replied. We placed our putters back in our golf bags and jumped into the golf cart. We began to make our way up the steepest hill in the entire golf course, which lead us to the eighth hole, a 150-yard par 3. We hopped out of the cart and grabbed our appropriate clubs for the hole. Rich was up first. He took his usual 100 practice swings and then finally approached the little white ball sitting on the tee. He began his swing and there it went! Slicing right, like a missile into the woods. Branches were falling everywhere while tons of birds and a few deer began to run and fly for cover. "Holy ****, Rich!" I said. "Wow! It's just not my day," he said, while laughing. We both shared a good chuckle and now it was my turn on the tee box. "I don't think I'm going to do much better here. The way we've both been playing here today, I wouldn't be surprised if I join you for a party of two in those woods," I said jokingly. I placed my ball on the tee, took a step back to look towards the green, which I could barely see with the sun shining right into our eyes. "I don't think you'll need to watch where this one goes, but just in case I do hit it straight, can you keep your eyes on the ball for me," I said to Rich. "Sure, no problem," he answered, while laughing. I took my swing and there it went! "I see it, I see it. Nice shot! That's going right at the flag stick," Rich said. I saw the ball hit the green, took a hop and then disappear! "Where did it go?" I asked Rich. "I don't know! I saw it hit once and then disappear! Let's go and take a look!" Rich replied. We hopped into the cart and made our way down to the green. We began to look around the perimeter of the green and in the sand traps. "I don't see it anywhere. You don't think it went in the hole, do you?" I asked Rich. "I don't know, let's take a look," he replied. We both made our way to the flag stick and peaked into the cup, and there it was! "Oh my God! I got a hole in one!" I screamed. We began to high-five and hug as if we just won a million dollars.

The rest of the round of golf was just a blur and I couldn't wait until I told my mom what had happened. We finished our round and there was that green Astro van sitting in the parking lot. I was moving so fast but I felt as if I was walking in slow motion. I opened the side door, took my seat in the back and Rich jumped into the front next to my mom. "So, how did it go, guys?" my mom asked. "Well, we played like garbage, but...Sean here got a hole-in-one!" Rich said. I was smiling from ear to ear, anxiously awaiting my mother's response. I knew she was going to be ecstatic and jumping out of her seat. "Oh, that's nice. What do you guys want to do for dinner?" she said, without any hesitation. I couldn't believe it! Rich then whipped his head left at her, amazed at her response. "Mom, you do know what that is, right?" Rich asked. "I believe so. It's when you make it in the right amount of times on that particular hole?" she answered with hesitation. Rich began to laugh and explain to her what it actually means to get a hole-in-one. She then pulled the car over, celebrated with extreme joy, looked back and gave me the biggest smile ever.

On the job, This is a big deal. I have to make sure this looks really nice, I said to myself as I was kneeling on a cold concrete floor. I had a torch in one hand and solder in the other, ready to make art out of copper. It was the first time my father had left me alone on a job all by myself and I was ready to prove to him that I was fully capable of doing it. I was assembling a main 1¼ copper water line, with a regulator, ball valves and hopefully a beautiful manifold setup for a public restroom in the town park. Each solder joint was done perfectly, the spacings between each copper tee were exactly the same, which was beautifully supported by bracket straps with threaded rod. When it was all said and done, it was truly a work of art! Time that day flew by so fast since I was now actually doing the hands on work, rather than assisting my fellow co-workers. Before I knew it, it was the end of the day, and I heard my father's truck pull up to the job. I made my final last-minute touch-ups, swept up the hardened solder mounds on the floor, and positioned the drop lights towards the piece of art I had created. I will never forget that moment when my father walked into that utility room. He smiled from ear to ear, gave me a slap on the back and said, "Looks great, Sean! Nice and level, neat and secure. Great job!"

When my father spoke those words, it was worth the hard work and effort that went into creating that plumbing masterpiece. Still to this day, my father will share his thoughts and feelings on each of our plumbing performances, both good and bad. His response gave me the confidence in my plumbing abilities and I was now ready to take anything on! I now try as much as I can to apply my father's enthusiasm towards my fellow co-workers and apprentices. We all as human beings want to feel important and to be praised for things we've done right or well. There is no better feeling in the world than hearing someone say, "Great work. Nice job. I'm proud of you." It's amazing to me though how difficult it can be for some people to actually say those words of encouragement. We all are quick to talk bad about people and their flaws. However, when it comes to praising someone for their hard work and accomplishments, we tend to shy away. I'm sure many of you who are reading this now can say they fall under that category. I encourage those people to step out of their comfort zones and give that employee some praise. That particular employee may feel he or she has accomplished something great, high-fiving themselves because they are so proud and all they want to hear is, "Great job. Nice work," and get a pat on the back. There is nothing worse than feeling as though you accomplished something great and not getting the praise you anticipated and deserved. Try it sometime and I guarantee you will see a major shift in that person's energy and work ethic.

New Year's Makeover

There I was staring down at the very healthy spread of hors d'oeuvres which lay in front of me on top of the fold-away table. Hmm, do I want some pigs in a blanket? Maybe stuffed mushrooms? Taco dip smothered in cheese with Doritos? Or a beautiful colorful spread of vegetables with a low fat Greek Yogurt dip? I asked myself. I grabbed my paper plate and loaded it up with all of the above, minus the veggies. I made my way outside to the beer cooler, grabbed a cold one and my night was ready to begin. I surveyed the room and began my usual New Year's Eve chit-chat sessions. "So, have any New Year's resolutions?" I inquired. Every response was pretty much the same. Go on a diet, stop smoking and exercise more. At least that's what I think I remember was being said, because I was in the zone chowing down on my delicious 'healthy' food. The night went on with more chit-chat, drinking, partying and laughter. The big ball dropped, confetti sprayed the air, horns blew in my ears and before I knew it, the sun was glowing on my face. I was ready to nurse my lovely hangover. I covered my head with my pillow and thought to myself, This is definitely no way to start out a new year!

It's amazing how many people are in my very same situation each New Year's Day. I am in no way saying you shouldn't drink, eat, laugh and have some fun. However, starting a new year in bed isn't the best way to kick things off! Don't be like the average New Year's Day person starting a new year feeling miserable. Let's be honest, we've ALL been there before! Switch it up this year and get your business off to a great start! As my fellow Phc News Columnist Ellen Rohr always says, hit the ground running! Plumber's wife turned business makeover expert, I pulled my seat up to the computer with my coffee in hand, becoming anxious and nervous as my wife and I waited for the first session to begin with Ellen. "Hello! Good morning, Sean and Azure! It's Ellen!" she said. I thought, Wow! This woman has some serious energy. I like it! Mind you, it's 7:00a.m. Eastern Standard Time and where Ellen is, its 6:00a.m.! I quickly sat up in my seat looked at my wife Azure, smiled and nodded. It was go time! The two-hour session was over before we knew it, and my wife and I were ready to conquer anything! It was my wife's first time diving into the family business, and she was ready to take on the responsibilities of the bookkeeping for BMC Plumbing. My wife and I were somewhat reluctant at first when we signed up with Ellen. However, that quickly changed the moment we spoke with her. She instilled confidence in my wife and I and after that first call, we were on a high! We first began our business meeting with Ellen back in April 2014 and we are just about finishing up with her now in January.

I can't begin to tell you how helpful she has been for BMC Plumbing and Heating. We understand more about bookkeeping and financials than we ever could imagine. For all of you out there who think, "I don't need help in this department of my business. My secretary and I are doing just fine," trust me guys, there is always room for improvement in your company. I am always in the field working with my hands and I still learn something new every day. I can't believe how much I've learned thus far about our financial situation in the office. It has made our company much more aware of where our money is being made and where we are spending it. If there is one thing to add to your New Year's resolution list this year, it's picking up that phone or hopping onto the computer and contacting Ellen Rohr.   So, in a nutshell, what am I suggesting here in this chapter? Don't   drink alcohol or eat horrible food?   No, enjoy it! However, when it comes to your plumbing, heating or HVAC Company this New Year, try something new. Get a fresh start and a new beginning.   I think contacting Ellen is a wonderful, smart way to hit the ground running this year. Instead of going through your same old routines, shake away that business hangover, bypass those greasy foods and pick up those veggies instead!

The Love of my Life

PRIDE. This is the one word that comes to mind when I think about my truck. Taking pride in one's truck goes a long way in the Plumbing and Heating industry. Yes, keeping it clean and organized is one thing, however, keeping on top of a shiny, attractive, well-functioning truck is another ball game. Each morning when I rise and step into my truck, I take a deep breath, exhale and smile. This is my office, my home away from home and I love it! A lot of trucks in the field get abused day in and out and it disgusts me greatly. Some people have no respect for their truck and neglect it completely. This drives me crazy!! I preach constantly to fellow co-workers and friends in the field how important it is to keep on top of your truck's condition. This machine you sit in every day makes you money while taking you from job to job, so start taking PRIDE in your office on wheels.

Finding "The One"

There she was, sitting in the lot, the most beautiful one of all. She was tall, shiny and gorgeous! I fell in love instantly! I just had to have her, the truck that is. The Nissan NV 3500 is the truck I fell in love with and now, several years later, I am still head over heels about her. Attention all contractors: You need to get this truck! This truck is one of a kind, with plenty of space, height and drives like luxury. I knew it was time to upgrade my vehicle after several bruises to my lower back from constantly hunching over and hitting my back on the roof! Enough was enough. Let's face it guys, the typical van is no longer a player anymore. The high roof truck is the way to go. Being able to walk into my truck and stand up while looking for a tool or fitting is such a great feeling! But don't take my word for it, try it out yourselves! Remember, nothing out there can compete with the Nissan NV trucks! Go out and search for "the one" and tie the knot that will change your plumbing life!

Office on Wheels

Let's face it; a lot of our work day is spent right in that truck. Either making phone calls, writing up an invoice or driving to that next job. The cockpit of the truck is your office on wheels. One of the most important selling points of my Nissan NV was the cockpit, from the overhead compartments to store additional work clothes and maps and the middle console where I keep my binders, folders and my laptop. I have everything I need in the cockpit that any other office would provide. I found that keeping an organized front of truck area helps to save time and money. This is definitely something to strongly consider, if or when you're looking for a new vehicle.

Routine Check Up.

One way to destroy and damage your truck is not to take care of it. It is so crucial to keep on top of oil changes every three months and get a car wash every other week. There is nothing like a nice shiny looking truck driving around from job to job. Little things like this will keep your truck young and healthy.

Double – Take

There is no better feeling in the world than seeing the double-take in action. This is where PRIDE in your truck begins to show. You know you have an attractive truck when you're getting everyone's attention on the main strip. I don't know about you but seeing a clean, well maintained truck tells me, this company is professional. I would be quicker to call the company with a nice new shiny truck, than an old, dirty, beat-up truck. Your truck is your billboard on wheels! Everywhere you drive, people see your logo and company name on that truck. The more professional it looks, the more the phone will be ringing off the hook. Trust me.

In and Out

I have climbed over mounds of tools and pipe throughout my plumbing career. It's the worst! Opening the back doors and looking into the junkyard is not a pleasant feeling! Having the right truck with plenty of room and shelving is the way to go! Going in and out of a truck for tools and fittings shouldn't be dangerous and I shouldn't be breaking a sweat! Getting yourself or your apprentice quickly in and quickly out of the well-organized truck will help save time and money.

Your relationship with your truck is a reflection of yourself and what your company stands for. It may not seem like much to maintain your vehicle and keep it shiny and new, but people do notice. If the customer sees that you have great PRIDE in your truck; they will certainly know your PRIDE for your truck will carry over to your work ethic. So go out there and find that "one", settle down, tie the knot and treat her with respect and care, the truck that is...

Sean McCormack

The Good. The Bad. The Ugly.

As my father always told me, "No one is perfect, especially when it comes to plumbing." Every plumber has their bad days and sometimes we must stop and have a good laugh at ourselves! Let's be honest guys, we've all done something on the job that leads us to say, "I can't believe what I just did!" Whether it's installing a pump the wrong way or installing a shower body upside down, it's certainly not our proudest moments, but it happens! Its times like these I enjoy talking to other plumbers about the bad and the ugly because I know I'm not the only one out there who's had the old brain fart from time to time! However, when chatting with fellow plumbers about our own silly mistakes, somehow the conversation ALWAYS leads to the great "Plumbers Bloopers" conversation, and we all have some great stories to tell, especially what we end up finding in those porcelain thrones! Here are a few of my favorite stories...

The Irish Surprise!

The day after St. Patrick's Day was a slow and sluggish day due to all of the food and drink that was had by all the night before! As I was wrapping up for work, I got a call that came in from my neighbor asking if I could swing by before heading home because his toilet wasn't flushing properly. I arrived to his front door ready for an easy snake job assuming they used too much double ply toilet paper. My neighbor Dan answered the door and directed me into the main bathroom where the problem existed. I asked him the usual questions, "How long has this been going on for? When did you use it last? Do you use double ply toilet paper? DID ANYTHING FALL INTO THE TOILET????" He replied, "It has been going on for about a day. I used it briefly this morning. I do use double ply and without a doubt, nothing fell into the toilet!" For some reason, I wasn't convinced with his last answer, given that he looked away and didn't seem very confident with his reply. So I went out to the truck and grabbed the snake. With the snake half way into the toilet, I started to hit a lot of resistance. I then backed the snake out and repeated this several times with the same result. After about 10 minutes, Dan walks back in and asks, "Any luck"? I turned and said, "Not yet, I'm hitting something that's pretty solid. Are you sure nothing fell down this toilet, Dan?" He then replied, "No. Hold on, let me ask my wife. Hey HUN! Nothing fell down this toilet, right?" His wife comes in and with a confused look on her face says, "I don't believe so, Dan, but, I mean last night we had some people over and got pretty rowdy, so anything is possible," in a joking manner. I decided to give it another shot, but still no luck! At this point, I did not feel like pulling the toilet to see if there was something that could be stuck! But, that's what had to be done. So I did. I pulled the toilet, turned in upside down, took my flashlight and shined it up the trap of the toilet. There they were…TWO WHOLE RED POTATOES! I couldn't believe my eyes! After much laughter and confusion coming from both parties, I managed to scoop out those potatoes and got their toilet functioning properly again. I didn't ask them how or why, but I certainly couldn't eat potatoes for a long time after that…

Thanksgiving Soup

Two days after Thanksgiving, I was still experiencing a food hangover and ready to wrap up the long work day, go home and take a much needed nap! We just had one more call to attend to and before long, I would be home and sleeping! So we arrive at the job to find the problem consisted of a faulty sewer ejector pump (NOT MY FAVORITE). So we got to the tank and began to back off the bolts that hold down the tank lid. Once we got the lid off, we took a look into the pit and saw a Thanksgiving Dinner in its liquid form! Ugh...let's just say there was a lot of corn! So, not wanting to reach down into the tank to pull the old pump out, I ran to the truck to get a cup and a bucket. I began to scoop the sewage into the bucket until the bucket was about full. I asked myself, "Now where do I dump this bucket full of Thanksgiving love?" The woods it was! So I grabbed the handle of the fully loaded bucket and began to walk into the woods at a very swift pace! About a quarter of the way through the woods, the fully loaded bucket hit a big rock and what followed wasn't pleasant! It was as if someone dropped a bowling ball into the bucket of sewage! SPLASH! All over my face and onto my clothing! NOT GOOD! I stood there in disbelief and ran to the truck for a few rags as I tried my best not to open my mouth. I managed to clean up the best I could and finished the job quickly! The smell was SO bad I took desperate measures. Before I jumped into the truck, I took some ABS glue and smeared it all over my clothing! I know, bad right? I had to do something and ABS glue was the first thing I could think of to disguise the wonderful smell of Thanksgiving Soup. It was a long ride home and a very long shower was taken...

Holy Cow!!

It was a Wednesday afternoon when I received a phone call from one of my customers Mary. I had answered and she said, "I have a problem up here in unit 103, there is water coming out of one of the light fixtures on the ceiling! I believe there's water coming from the unit upstairs, apartment #203!" I said, "I'm on my way up!" I was around the corner working in my office so I shot up to unit 203 right away! I arrived and as soon as I entered the bathroom, I found a toilet stoppage. I had my plunger in one hand and a closet auger in the other. I saw no evidence of what might have caused the problem so I ran the auger down and I had a bite in a few seconds! Mary asked, "What is it??" I said, "I have no clue but it's very big!" So I began to pull on it and eventually the object became visible near the top of the toilet, when Mary then shouted, "Oh my God!! What the heck is that!!?" I said, "Here, hold this so I can grab it!" As Mary came over to assist me, it jumped off and went back down the toilet! We both looked at each other with confusion and concern written all over our face. I said, "This looks like an eel or something!" She began laughing and I quickly got prepared for a second dive in with the snake! I ran the auger again quickly hoping it didn't escape! GOTCHA! I pulled like crazy as if I was out on the lake fishing! It came up and I grabbed that sucker, pulled it out and threw it on the floor! Mary began to scream, "Oh My God! Stomp on it!" I was ready to stomp, but realized what it was! It was a full beef tongue!! "Ugh! Mary," I said, "how did this beef tongue get into this toilet!?? She looked just as confused as I was! It was rotten and stunk to high heaven!

Sometimes, I wonder how these things end up finding themselves down those toilets!!

Con-DUMB!

It was an early Monday morning call that came through about a backed up toilet. I called the customer back and said I'd be right over. I arrive at the house and the husband answers the door with a nervous, awkward hello. "Hi, hey, umm… yeah, come on in." He began to look around very nervously, as his son was attached to his leg begging him to come back inside to play with his toys. "Hang on pal," he said, "I'll be right in. I just have to show the plumber to the bathroom." So we began our climb up the stairs and eventually reached the bathroom. I thought to myself, Why is this guy acting so weird! He must have clogged that toilet and maybe he's really embarrassed. It's really no big deal. So I began to snake out the toilet as the homeowner was watching over my shoulder like a hawk! I ran the snake in one time and BINGO! That wonderful sound of a clogged toilet sucking down like no tomorrow! Just as I got the toilet unclogged, the wife had entered the bathroom asking what caused the clog. The husband quickly butted in and asked his wife to please go downstairs and that everything was under control. She refused and stayed in the bathroom to watch along with her nosey husband. I backed out the snake and there it was! A condom! I said, with laughter, "Well, here's your culprit!" As I lifted my head, I saw the husband with a cherry-red face, ready to strangle me and a wife ready to strangle him! "Hmmm, that's strange, STEVE. I wonder how that got into the toilet?? SWE DON'T USE PROTECTION!" I was at a loss for words...She quickly stormed out of the bathroom and into her room which was followed by an earth shattering SLAM from the bedroom door. I quickly got my tools together and said, "I'm very sorry! I will go now and we'll be in touch..."

Surprise!

It was a cold afternoon as my father and I sat in his truck. The only thing keeping me warm was the steam coming off from my cup of piping hot green tea. My father and I were discussing how amazing nature was and how incredible the squirrels were as they began to frantically run around looking for nuts and prepping a nest right above us in a big pine tree. I was amazed how fast the little creatures could move! As I sat there mesmerized by these incredible creatures, I could feel as if my father wanted to discuss something. I was hesitant to ask because usually when I get these vibes from my father, it's because I've done something terribly wrong! Just as the thought crossed my mind, he spoke, "You know, Sean. I was thinking of throwing a surprise party for mom next month." Phew! I thought to myself. "Oh yeah, that sounds like fun," I said. My father continued, "Yeah, mom is turning the big 5-0 and I think she deserves a nice party!" Knowing that my mom hated to be surprised, I was going to say something, but I choose not to. "I'm going to invite..." as my father started listing all of these people which accumulated quickly. "Wow, that's going to be a lot of people, dad. You sure mom is going to be okay with having such a big party?" I asked, and trying to hint that maybe we should re-evaluate the idea of a big surprise party. "Oh yeah. Mom will be fine. She will enjoy celebrating with all of the people she loves! What's the worst that could happen?" he said. I simply nodded and said, "Well, worst case scenario dad, is that she'll slap you, but if it's something you want to do, let's start planning!" Before we knew it, there we were at the restaurant frantically setting up balloons, center pieces and pictures in a room filled with people! Then my phone vibrated in my sweaty palms! It was the text message saying they have arrived. "Everyone! Everyone! The eagle has landed! Please be quiet!" I shouted. In a matter of seconds, the room became incredibly silent as we all stood there staring at the double doors which lead into the room. All we could hear were muffled noises from the hostess as the voices drew closer and closer. "Shhh! Shhh! Here she comes." The doors opened slowly and there she was! "SURPRISE!!!" She jumped back with her eyes wide open and her hands over her mouth. She immediately turned to my father and began to playfully slap him a few times while my father put his guard up as he was well aware that "worst case scenario" beating was now in full effect…

As I've always said, every day is a school day when it comes to plumbing and heating. On this one day with a particular customer of ours, I once again learned something very valuable. This customer was having trouble with their hot water boiler as it was leaking from the relief valve. I entered the boiler room, setup my drop light and got a look at the problem. "Well, it looks as if your pressure in the boiler is high. The reason for this leak out of the relief valve is because your expansion tank here is shot." I said this with great confidence. "I will only need to throw a new expansion tank in here as well as a relief valve." She nodded and said, "Alright, sounds good, I'll let you do your thing!" To make a long story short, I replaced the expansion tank and relief valve which only helped for a few days as the relief valve began to leak again! The problem was the faulty S-1156F, which was letting too much pressure into the boiler. I replaced that and two weeks later, the boiler began to leak again! I couldn't believe it! What I should have done was the following, "Well, what's happening here is the pressure in your boiler is high, which causes this relief valve to leak. Here is what we suggest when this happens. We would like to replace the following, the S-1156F, expansion tank, relief valve and air cans if need be. However, it seems that this boiler has seen better days. I can replace all of these parts for you and you should be good to go. However, since this boiler is very old, I would suggest possibly changing it." By explaining this to the customer at that time, it would have saved me some serious headaches! I was so confident in what I was doing back then, but it bit me in the butt in the long run. I should have explained this "worst case scenario" to the customer, which I do now! It gives them something to think about and puts the ball in the customer's court. Nine times out of ten, the customer's not going to know what's going on with the boiler and how long it has to live. By explaining to them the different options, costs and worst case scenarios, it can save you and the customer in the long run! I feel by taking the time to explain the plumbing problem at hand and giving the customer the options up front, this will only save you from headaches down the road. The last thing you want is a beat down from a customer, like the one my father got from my mom that surprise party afternoon...

Do You Believe In Ghosts?

"Mission complete, dad. Toilet is in, looking good. No leaks. No runs. No errors," I said to my father over the phone. "Perfect! Head over to 25 North Franklin Street. We have a doozy of a hot water heater installation over there," my father said. A doozy? I'm sure it won't be that bad, I thought to myself. I arrived at the job and was greeted by Dan, the carpenter. "Hi, Sean. You ready for a challenge? I hope you're not afraid of tight, dark, spooky crawl spaces," he said. I laughed, shrugged my shoulders and said, "Nah, I've pretty much seen it all. Let's have a look!" Boy, oh boy, Dan wasn't kidding when he said it was a tight spot! "This might require a little Duck Butter action in order to squeeze her into this space," I said, jokingly. After much swearing and some laughter, we managed to literally squeeze the 40-gallon low boy heater into the confines of the dungeon. "Any ghosts in there, Sean?" Dan said as he stuck his head into the opening of the crawl space. I gave a good chuckle and replied, "Nope, no ghosts in here!" "Did I ever tell you about the time I was working at an old farmhouse upstate?" Dan asked. "No, you didn't," I replied. Then, I began to wonder if I wanted to hear this after all. Just as the thought crossed my mind, Dan began his story. "Yeah, we were finishing some work, and toward the end of the day, I'd swear I saw something from the corner of my eye at the top of the staircase," he explained. "I looked upstairs, and of course there was nothing there. About 10 minutes later, I passed the staircase again and looked up, but a bit more reluctantly. This time I saw a ghost-like figure staring down at me. No joke, Sean—I literally freaked out! I packed up my belongings and headed for the front door as fast as I could," he said. He continued, "I found out I wasn't the only one who had seen the ghost. Other workers on the job saw her, and the neighbors told us many people have seen the same ghost throughout the years. I spent the entire week looking over my shoulder." OK, great, I thought to myself. Now I was spooked. I looked warily around the crawl space, certain that a ghost was going to materialize at any moment. Needless to say, these were probably the quickest solder joints I've done in a long time. Throughout my plumbing career, I've been in some creepy homes and foreboding basements. One house in particular, which was built back in the early 1800s, was probably the most disconcerting of them all. I arrived at the job, looked over the lengthy to-do list left by the homeowner and began to plumb away. I made my way to the stairwell, which led to the second floor, and I began my climb with tool bucket in hand. Each step produced an eerie creak and the spiral stone wall, which followed me to my left, gave off a cold, damp feel. I knew I was the only one in the house, but nonetheless, I began to feel as if I might not be alone after all. From the top of the staircase, I made my way down the low-lit hallway, where dusty pictures of random, strange-looking people were on display. As I walked, the wood floor creaked louder and louder. I called out nervously, "Hello, anyone here?" Thankfully, there was no answer. After assuring myself it was just my imagination, I made my way to the bathroom. I stood in the tub and began to take off the old American Standard shower trim, since the stems and seats were defective. As I was doing this, I kept hearing eerie noises I could not recognize and what sounded like a door creaking very slowly. I didn't want to get out of the tub, but I knew I had to make my way downstairs to the basement in order to shut down the main water supply. Sean, stop being silly, I told myself. There is no one here but you. I made my way downstairs to the basement to shut the ball valve and scuttled quickly back upstairs. I got back in the tub and began to change the stems on the shower body, all the while looking out into the hallway to be absolutely sure there was no one there. Of course, there wasn't, but I couldn't shake the feeling that I was being watched the whole time. I began to work at a much faster pace, moving quickly through the house, fixing all of the things on my list. In the end, I managed to get out of that house alive to tell the story! Although I never actually saw a ghost in that spooky house, I know for sure there was someone or something keeping a close eye on me. I could feel I was being watched and it gave me chills the entire time I was there. I know I'm not the only plumber out there who's had supernatural encounters on the job. I would like to hear some of your spooky stories. Have you ever seen a ghost while on the job? Do you believe in ghosts?

Get Fit to Fit

I really hope it's only 3:00a.m. right now. I still need at least three more hours of sleep, I said to myself as I lay in my nice, warm, cozy bed.

I knew my alarm was set for 6:05a.m., as it was for every week night, and I didn't want to ruin my "beauty sleep" by picking up my head and glancing at the cable box at the foot of the bed. So, I nestled into my warm comforter and began to doze off again, enjoying every minute that went by. My sleep was quickly disturbed by a warm, smelly breath, followed by a cool, slimy "goo" that dripped onto my right cheek.

Please, Norman, go back to sleep, I thought to myself. I pulled the blanket back over my ears and tried to get some sleep. Norman had stopped panting and decided to move to the end of the bed, where he circled for a minute and eventually laid back down.

"Yes, now I can finally get some sleep," I said.

I reluctantly picked up my head and opened one eye to glance at the cable box.

5:45a.m. Nice, I have 15 minutes before I need to get up and head to the gym, I thought. Just as my head hit the pillow, I was again awakened by the most unpleasant smell: bulldog pollution.

"OK, time to get up!" I said.

I swung my legs around and hopped out of bed and began to get ready for my workout. Shortly thereafter, I had a giant cup of coffee in my hand and was ready to take on the gym. Once my workout was complete, I was headed to my first job of the day. It was the one job I was not looking forward to at all. I had to go to Mrs. Smith's house and switch out a leaking kitchen sink faucet. The only twist is that this was not the first time I've been underneath her shoe box of a cabinet.

I made sure that morning I did extra stretching at the gym because I knew I was going be utilizing all of my yoga skills underneath that kitchen sink. So, I arrived and plugged in my drop light, opened up the cabinet doors and was quickly reminded of how tight this space really was. Oh yeah, I forgot to mention one small detail — there was a fully functioning, still very hot, radiator placed ever so perfectly inside the cabinet. I managed to slither my way into the tight spot and began to work on the faucet.

"Wow, Sean, good thing you are slim and flexible enough to get into that space," Mrs. Smith said, as she laughed. "You really have to be a contortionist to fit into some of these tight spots, huh?"

I laughed and thought to myself, If I had a dollar for every time a customer said that to me, I'd be rich!

Well, maybe not rich, but I would have at least enough money that I'd be able to afford a nice steak and wine dinner! After an hour or so of cursing under my breath and being burned by the hot drop light and the nice toasty radiator, the job was complete. This, of course, was not my first rodeo when it came to tight spots on the job site.

I'm sure many of you can relate to exactly what I'm talking about. I know that without taking good care of my body by watching what I eat and constantly going to the gym to start my day, that fitting into these tight areas would be a lot more difficult.

Now, I'm sure you're wondering where I'm going with this one, right? Well, I can preach to you about health and fitness and how important it is for your mind and body, and how crucial it is to take care of your body, especially in this industry. But, I'm not a professional in the fitness field. However, I do have a good friend and customer of mine, Christina Hernandez who has been a health coach for three years and is a group fitness instructor on her way to being an ACSM Certified Personal Trainer. She says she hasn't always loved health and fitness. But once she made the choice to lead a healthier life, she never looked back because the benefits were endless: controlling weight, gaining flexibility, improving moods, combating illness/disease, boosting energy and improving longevity are just naming a few.

Christina wants to pass more information forward and teach others about the benefits of a healthy diet, exercise and having a positive mental attitude. She shared some tips with me that I would like to pass on to you.

Tip No. 1

It is important when starting any new goal or project to have a reason why you are doing it. Why do you want to be healthier? Is it because you want to do better at your job? Run around with your kids more? Be able to do more with your spouse? Have more energy? Look healthier and fit? Finding a "why" is the most important step because that is what will keep you going when you feel like quitting. Another important thing is believing in yourself. There is that famous quote, "If you believe you can, you're right. If you believe you can't, you're right." You control the outcome in every situation, so you need to be positive and believe you can do anything you set your mind to. Nobody has more motivation than you; not the person next to you or someone on Facebook. You are your own motivation, and if you want it, you have to light the fire within you and put in the work. Christina said to always remember that it's easier not to do something than it is to do it, but lots of people don't do it, and look what's happening to the nation's overall health.

Tip No. 2

So now that you have the correct mindset about having a healthier life, let's go over some of the main concepts. Rest is super important. Regular periods of rest and sleep are vital to our personal well-being. Being sleep deprived is dangerous and limits our ability to do things like operate heavy machinery and drive, and can also weaken immune systems and make you ill. Of course, everyone's sleep patterns are different, but Christina says getting anywhere from seven to eight hours a night is good for mental health, healing your body, letting muscle groups recuperate, and fighting illness.

Tip No. 3

"Bad food, diet and nutrition are at an epidemic level in this country," Christina said. We love food and we love it fast and easy, but it's not always healthy that way, is it?

The phrase, "you are what you eat" may be cliché, but it's ultimately accurate. Obesity, high cholesterol levels, high blood pressure and Type II Diabetes are all common problems. Christina said they are often a direct result of a poor diet. Modern diets can contain too many processed foods that are high in fats, sugar and salt. We know that we should be eating more lean meat, fresh fruit, and vegetables as a part of a healthy diet.

Simple changes to your diet can make a big difference to your life, including increasing your energy levels, enhancing your mood and reducing the occurrence of illness. Christina advises portioning meals and eating many meals throughout the day. Many of us overeat at mealtimes and that causes us to gain weight. By serving yourself the correct foods like vegetables, fruits and lean proteins, and giving yourself the correct portion size, you can eliminate over-eating the wrong foods. As they say, "You can't out exercise a bad diet."

Tip No. 4

Last, but not least important, is exercise. Most people are aware of the advice that we should take regular exercise, but many people like to say that they don't have time. Everybody has the same amount of time, but not everyone makes the time. Christina suggests you think of it as an appointment with yourself. You wouldn't miss an appointment with a client, so you should show up for yourself and your own health too.

Christina recommends that people exercise at least three times a week for a minimum of 30 minutes. Some people like going to the gym. Christina works out at home either in the living room, driveway or on a deck. She knows that she will not get up to drive to the gym every day so she just writes down a circuit workout, goes for a run or pops in a workout DVD like INSANITY to get it done in 30 minutes. Other people love going to the gym or taking different classes because being in that environment works better for them and helps them get motivated.

Christina warned that if you have an injury, you should consult a physician or modify your workouts; everyone has been there. Everyone is different and should do what works best for them in terms of time management and workout preference. If you can't work out as much as Christina recommends, then do what you can because nobody has yet concluded that exercise is bad for you and the only bad workout is the one you didn't do.

No matter what, it is important to ease yourself gently into any new routine whether it's incorporating a new diet or exercise regiment, or both. Caring for your body is the best thing that you can do for yourself. Christina likes to reward herself at certain milestones whether it's pounds lost, running a faster mile, doing more pushups, etc. She will have a "treat meal," purchase new sneakers, start a new workout program, get a new yoga mat, etc. to motivate her to keep going. Christina said you won't be able to do the right thing all the time, but with practice, you will get better at making sure you take care of your body, get the most out of life, and, as plumbers, fit in all the right places!

Get started!

Thank you, Christina for sharing your knowledge and expertise in the health and fitness field! I feel it's so important for us plumbers to take care of our bodies because every day we find ourselves lifting heavy materials and fitting into these tight spots. Let's face it, this industry can be very taxing on your mind and body, so let's do our bodies a favor and take good care of them.   For more motivational tips on eating healthy and working out, follow Christina on social media: Instagram-Mrs.Motivation; Facebook - Christina Hernandez-Inspire. Motivate. Empower; and Twitter - The_ChristinaH.

Incentives for Choc. Chip Pancakes

"Well Sean, it's either you or me who has to sneak behind that tight boiler and make that repair. Since I'm the one climbing up those extension ladders because you're afraid of heights, I vote you squeeze behind this nice boiler here," Glenn said. "Not a problem! These tight spots, cockroaches spider webs and crawl spaces are no problem for me, just as long as you keep marching up those ladders when need be," I said. So, I jokingly began my stretching and started to maneuver my way between the boiler and hot water heater. As I pushed through, I had to inhale in order for my waist and stomach to fit. I'm sure all of you reading this right now know exactly what I'm talking about. Once past the boiler and hot water heater, I finally made my way back to a cold, concrete wall. I then had to slip under some copper piping and bend my head awkwardly to the side to avoid contact with the still very warm flu piping. "OK, I have a visual on the zone valve," I said. "OK, are you nice and comfy in there?" Glenn asked. "I would have it no other way, Glenn. I'll take this any day over sitting at a desk bored out of my mind," I replied. Glenn began to hand me the drop light and all of my necessary tools to begin my procedure of splicing out an old Honeywell zone valve. I was hoping it was the newer model Honeywell zone and I could just replace the zone head and be in and out of there. But, of course, the one zone on the entire boiler which was placed ever so perfectly in the back turned out to be the type I had to drain the entire heating system in order to sweat in a new zone. Nonetheless, I began the work at hand to make the proper repair. "So, how are the boys doing?" I asked. "They are doing great actually! Quinn (his son) is playing hooky today with Jenny (wife) because he had earned a 92 percent on his exam in school. They are headed into town for lunch at his favorite restaurant and then going to play some bowling." "Wow, that's great you guys do that for the kids, Glenn. If my parents did that for me, I definitely would have scored higher grades on my exams," I said jokingly.

As I was soldering the last joint, the thought came to me. Why don't we use incentives for our co-workers when it comes to selling and performing well on the job? Let's be honest now, either when you were a child or if you are now a mother or father of your own children, there was at least one time or another you were offered some kind of incentive or had offered an incentive to your children. I remember it like it was yesterday — my parents said if I behaved in Sunday morning church, that my brothers, sisters and I would go out to Perkins Restaurant for pancakes. And let me tell you, we were on our best behavior every Sunday morning because all we could think about were those delicious chocolate chip fluffy pancakes! It is amazing to me how well children and adults react and respond to an intriguing incentive. So you have to ask yourself, why wouldn't this work with your business?

My father and I took action just recently this summer and began to create an incentive or an upsell sheet for ourselves and our employees. On the sheet of paper, we listed all of the things we could upsell to our customers while in their homes; pressure regulator, boiler, hot water heater, toilet packages, etc. And for each upsell, the workers would take note of what they sold to that customer and keep a tally throughout the month. For each additional part or product they sold, they would receive a cash incentive. It's amazing how much we all now are trying to upsell in times where we didn't before. Of course, you are not going to walk into Mrs. Smith's house on a toilet flapper repair and start selling her on a new boiler in the middle of the summer. You have to be a little more creative than that. I'll give you an example that happened last week. A customer of ours called about a leaky bathroom faucet and wanted us to stop over and take a look. So, I shot over there, assessed the situation and found that the basin faucet was on the old side, and it was a cheap Home Goods special. I explained to the customer that instead of replacing the stems to the faucet, I felt it would be in her best interest to replace the faucet with a better quality product. I also explained to her that she may have a pressure issue in the house. I told her, "Faucets usually begin to leak when the pressure is high, which is no different than blood pressure in your body. When your blood pressure is high, it puts a lot of strain on your organs. The same principle applies with your water pressure and your fixtures, being the organs of the house." This is where I usually get that "wow, interesting" look on their faces. So, now I have sold her on the basin faucet package on our list and I'm headed downstairs to check the pressure. The pressure was very high, which leads to me changing the regulator. And while in the basement, I was able to get my eyeballs on her hot water heater and boiler and throw a couple of stickers on them. Before we had our company's incentive program, I may not have sold the regulator, or for that matter, the upgraded basin faucet. The company was now making extra money, and I had some extra cash in my pocket at the end of the month to take the family out for a nice dinner.

I would like for you to give this a shot and implement an incentive list into your company, even if you have to start small and eventually build up the list and incentives. It doesn't have to be cash. You can offer many things to catch your employees' attention. There's one thing I know for sure, regardless of the reward, I will not be stepping foot on those rickety extension ladders. Whatever it is you decide, I'm sure that you will see an enthusiasm you've never seen before from your workers and you will certainly start seeing an increase in your company's profit.

Sean McCormack

Huddle-Up Sundays

While I was lying in my warm, comfortable bed with a cool, crisp breeze blowing through the open window, I took a deep breath, stretched and thought to myself, I love the fall season.

Just as the thought crossed my mind, that wonderful aroma of coffee whipped past my nose and I quickly remembered, "It's football Sunday!"

It was the usual sleeping arrangements in our packed bed. My wife, son and dog, Norman, were all asleep, taking advantage of Sunday morning leisure. I had to make sure I got out of the bed without disturbing any of them. So, I ever so carefully lifted the comforter, slid my right leg out of the bed, and then continued to slither the rest of my body like a snake, making sure not to make much movement.

Yes, success! I thought to myself. I then slipped on my slippers, threw on a shirt, brushed my teeth, peeked back into the room to ensure there was not any movement, and then made

126

my way down the hallway to the living room. Football Sundays are one of my favorite days of the week. It's a time where I truly believe I am a NFL owner because of Fantasy Football.

For all of you who play Fantasy Football, you know exactly what I'm talking about. I picked up the remote, turned the channel to ESPN and grabbed my phone to look over my lineup. After 10 minutes of talking to myself and flipping through my lineup trying to decide who is going to get the start for the week, I made my way into the kitchen to grab a hot cup of coffee and make breakfast.

Sunday is not only my favorite day of the week because of football, but also because I am home with family and I get to prepare breakfast for them. Before I do anything, I take a big sip of my delicious coffee and preheat the oven for the best breakfast food of them all: BACON. Yes, that's right, I bake my bacon in the oven. If you haven't tried this technique, you must try this approach over frying it in the pan. Trust me!

Anyhow, I put the bacon on the baking sheet and placed the sheet into the oven. Not even 30 seconds later, I hear those nails hitting the hardwood floors getting closer to the kitchen. Yup, you guessed it. Norman the bulldog is always the first one awake when the smell of bacon is in the air.

With my lovely bulldog assistant in the kitchen drooling on the tile floor, I prepped my famous pancakes. I pulled out the eggs, milk, and butter, and when I closed the refrigerator door, standing there was chef No. 2, my son, Mason.

"Da-da, can I help you make pancakes?" Mason asked, as he was rubbing his eyes.

"Sure you can! Go pull up that chair and bring it next to me near the counter top," I said.

"Da-da, I want do the eggs this time, okay? Da-da, okay?" Mason asked.

"Not this time, Mason. But, I'll let you pour the milk and stir the mixture," I replied. After trying to negotiate with me, he eventually and reluctantly agreed, and we began to make our pancakes together. One would think that the aroma of buttery pancakes, coffee and bacon would wake anyone up. But think again, not Mama Bear. On Sunday mornings, I need to peel her off the bed. And rightfully so, as she is constantly on the move dealing with a 4-year-old 24/7 and is also expecting our second child. Nonetheless, eventually everyone sat down at the table and enjoyed our wonderful pancake breakfast. It was time for the best part of Sunday, watching football.

Boiler day

Although Sunday is one of my favorite days of the week, if I had to choose a working day that is at the top of my list, it would definitely have to be Boiler Day. I arrived at the job site early that Monday morning, ready to rip out an old beast in the basement and install a new masterpiece.

As all boiler jobs begin, our team walks through the house and starts to map out our entry and exit plans for the old and new boilers. Some of the houses that we work in are not the best for fitting and maneuvering large pieces of equipment. We are often puzzled how they were able to get the old boiler down into the basement, because it seems as if they built the house around the units.

I made my way down old rickety, creaky, wobbly basement stairs and set up shop for the day. I plugged in all the lights, brought in all of the necessary tools for dismantling, threw on a hose and drained the system. After the dismantling phase was complete, it was on to the most important time of the morning, breakfast! I'm sure you can guess by this time in the article what my favorite meal of the day is.

Breakfast wasn't like my family's Sunday extravaganza, but it was a good way for our team to socialize about life and catch up on all of the minor work-related issues over a hot cup of coffee and a muffin. After our pow wow session was over, it was time for the old and new units to exit and enter the house. We did our walk through again to ensure the best possible routes. This is where the mayhem and confusion started to happen.

At this point, there were about five or six workers, all having a say on what, where, when and how to accomplish the task. So after about 10 minutes of discussion, we came to a conclusion and began taking the old one out. Let's just say, 9 times out of 10, the "original" plan usually doesn't go accordingly. We had two guys counting to three at different times to plan each lift of the boiler, and we had guys trying to change the plan of attack midway up the flight of stairs. There is always confusion whenever we are faced with this task, and we are always so close to either damaging something or someone in the process. After dealing with this for a very long time, I had to do something about this problem and take some action.

Quarterback

While watching football on Sunday, I started to notice a trend in how quarterbacks perfected their trade. They all knew how to command, direct and control the huddle. The quarterback who stands out in particular is Drew Brees of the NFL's New Orleans Saints.

If you get a chance on Sunday, do yourself a favor and watch this man control the huddle. Each time the team huddles up, he gets down on one knee and makes eye contact with each player, making sure his teammates are listening and understanding his play call. You can see that his teammates respect him and his leadership abilities.

While watching Drew Brees command the huddle, I started to think, This is how BMC Plumbing needs to plan before boiler replacements. With any tasks at hand that you face out in the field that involves a team effort, you must take control of the situation. Grab your employees' attention and let them know that you are calling the plays. Could you imagine if while Drew Brees was in the huddle and his teammates were all shouting out what play should be run? It would be total mayhem, and just wouldn't work.

Well, the same applies in our industry. You cannot have co-workers shouting out and demanding different options, all while halfway up a staircase and lifting a 500-pound boiler. I use the boiler example in this chapter, but you can apply this to any part of your career. In order to take control of any situation at hand that is especially crucial, you must learn to take a stand, demand the attention from your audience and be the leader of the huddle. It's never good to have too many cooks in one kitchen. I hope you enjoyed this chapter on my breakfast rituals and the resulting work inspiration, and I would love to hear some of yours!

10X Your Life

It was a Sunday evening and my wife Azure, our son Mason and I had just finished up dinner at one of our favorite Italian restaurants. It had been a long day, which started with Mason waking up at 6:00a.m., bouncing up and down on our bed, wanting to get the day started early. I awoke all groggy — I just wanted to stay in bed and sleep. "C'mon, Dada! C'mon, Mama! Get up. Let's wake up and play," Mason yelled. I rolled over and looked at my wife as she gave me that "Oh my god" look. "OK, OK, OK, Mason. We are getting up," I said. I rolled out of bed and the day began. Mason came flying past me down the hallway, dove onto the couch and began to play with his toys. Oh my god, how does this kid have this much energy so early in the morning? I thought to myself. He was energized and ready to take on the day. From that moment on, for the rest of the day, it was non-stop action—from running outside playing soccer, to playing superheroes in the house and diving on the floors and furniture. Each step of the way, Mason would not only run around and play, but he would negotiate and sell me on his ideas and plans. "OK Mason, time to take a break now," I said. "What about we just play for five more minutes, Dada?" "No, I think we should take a small break and then we can play again after that," I answered. "How about we just play for four minutes then, Dada?" he countered quickly. I gave up. "OK, four minutes then," I replied. This went on all day with him, from taking playtime breaks to how many bites of food he needs to eat during lunch and dinner.

He was the king of negotiation in my house, selling me on his ideas and plans. The negotiating even continued on the car ride home from the restaurant. My wife and I laid out a plan for our bedtime routine, but he managed to rearrange the plans ever so slightly to gain one or two extra minutes of playtime before brushing his teeth and reading his books. He negotiated with us to the very last second his head hit the pillow before he fell asleep for the night. Kids like my son Mason have tremendous amounts of energy, day in and day out. They hop right out of bed and dive right into the day with extreme action. Mason knew exactly what his plan was on that Sunday and he conquered the day with energy, negotiating and selling us on his plans.

As plumbers, this is how we need to start living our lives out in the field. Whether we like it or not, we are salesmen. We are constantly in homes making repairs to problems at hand. Can you honestly say that when you enter a home, you are taking advantage of your full selling potential? I can't tell you how many times I've walked into a customer's house and simply repaired the problem at hand without suggesting some additional concerns or issues that should have been addressed. Now, I make an effort to get into the basement by offering a complimentary water pressure test, and I explain to the customer how important it is to maintain healthy pressure to ensure a longer lifespan for all of their fixtures. This allows me to scope out the hot water heater, pressure regulator and heating and cooling systems. If something looks questionable, I can then simply suggest to the customer the possible problems and solutions. Your goal from that point is to close the deal, negotiate and sell the customer on taking care of any other plumbing problem at hand.

Grant Cardone

This is very important for all you plumbers out there! Go to your nearest bookstore or online shopping website and purchase Grant Cardone's book, "The 10X Rule." I bought the audiobook last week (I prefer audio because I'm constantly in the truck every day) and I strongly suggest you do the same. I feel like I am feeding my brain information and positivity while I work. Grant Cardone is a king of motivation, and he knows how to sell! He has changed the way I live my life, how I run my company, and how I sell to my customers. He has taught me to apply that very same energy my son has day in and day out to my life. I now wake up early and spring out of bed ready to take on the day. It's so important to have that energy every day in your business and personal life. You will be surprised at how your positive energy will radiate to not only your co-workers, but also to your customers. I've never suggested you buy a particular book before, but please purchase this book, and others from Grant Cardone. Trust me, it will change your life. Now get into those basements and sell, sell, sell! Follow Grant Cardone on Periscope,   Twitter   and   SnapChat.   Search

@GrantCardone for all platforms. Tell him Sean the Plumber sent ya!

The Jazz Guru

"Well Sean, I have something to tell you," said Vinney, my drum instructor as he sat beside me getting ready to wrap up the lesson. "This unfortunately is going to be our last lesson with one another. I am starting a new career next week and it will be taking up all of my time. I just wanted to let you know that you are one of my favorite students and I think you have some real potential as a drummer." Man, this sucks, I thought to myself.

Vinney was this hip, cool Rock 'n Roll drummer and I'll never find another instructor out there like him. Just as the thought crossed my mind, Vinney said, "Now, just because I'm no longer going to teach you, I still want you to pursue another instructor and I have just the right person for you! He's a little older and he's not a Rock 'n Roll type drummer, however, you will teach you things that no one will ever be able to teach." He then reached down to his briefcase and pulled out his notepad and a pen and began to write in script the name of the gentleman that would supposedly teach me all I need to know about drums and technique. As he was writing, I couldn't help but think that maybe this was the end of taking lessons. After Vinney was done writing on the piece of paper that I knew would just end up in the garbage, he placed the paper down on my practice pad, took his drum stick and pointed at the paper and said, "This man will change your drumming world and bring your talent to the next level." I looked at him, smiled and said, "OK, I will give him a call," knowing full well I wasn't going to call him. Vinney then placed his hand on my shoulder and said his final goodbye speech, packed up his sticks, books and briefcase and made his way to the door. He then turned around and said, "By the way, he's big into jazz music. It's not like the Rock n' Roll we learn here together, but trust me, it will really help you with your chops."

The door closed behind Vinney and I said softly under my breath, "Jazz music? Why the hell would I want to learn how to play jazz? Help with my chops? I think I have pretty good technique already, and I'm a Rock 'n Roll drummer." I then starred down at the piece of paper, shook my head and stuck the piece of paper in my pocket. A few weeks went by and I would occasionally think about calling this jazz drum instructor by the name of Sonny Igoe. After much pondering, I thought, Maybe I'll just call him and see what he's all about. It can't hurt to give it a try. So, that next morning I grabbed the phone and began to dial Sonny's number. "Hello?" Sonny said. "Hi, Sonny? My name is Sean McCormack and I was referred to you by Vinney, my old drum instructor." "Vinney? I don't know a Vinney! What are you trying to sell me, sir?" he replied. "Uh, nothing. I was told to give you a call in regards to taking some lessons with you," I said. Then there was that eerie silence on the other end of the phone. "Hello?" I said. The next thing I heard was a very hardy and contagious laughter on the other end of the phone. "I'm just messing around with you, kid. I just want to make sure you have a good sense of humor before you decide to take some lessons with me. You can't always be so serious, you know" he said. I began to laugh and agreed with him. "So, I'm free Sunday morning at 6:00a.m. It's an hour lesson for $100. I will see you then?" he asked. I said, "Uh, Sunday? 6:00a.m.? Uh, yes, I will be there." "Great, bring a smile, a good attitude and, oh yeah, your drum sticks!" he said. Sunday morning I was awakened by my alarm clock at 5:20a.m. I reached for my alarm and lay back down. Jazz music? 5:30a.m.? What am I doing? Just get up and do this Sean, it may be all well worth it. So, up out of bed and got myself ready with all of my sticks, smiles and somewhat of a good attitude.

After about a half hour drive, I reached my destination and was let in through the backdoor by Sonny's wife.

"Sonny, Sean is here and he has a big smile on his face. So far so good!" she shouted down to Sonny. I made my way down the staircase and was greeted by an 80 year old, happy-go-lucky gentleman. He shook my hand and thanked me for coming by and told me to take a seat. I couldn't help but look around at all of the black and white photos hanging up in the studio and I began to realize that this guy was a big deal. We sat down at our practicing pads and he told me to pick up the drum sticks and just alternate the sticks by hitting the drum pad. I picked up the sticks and began to strike the drum pad, thinking to myself, This is odd. "OK, stop," he said. "We are going to start from the extreme basics of holding the drum stick and learning to strike the drum properly." He then picked up his sticks and began to demonstrate exactly what he wanted me to do. It seemed so basic to me, and I felt as if I was moving my potential in the opposite direction. Fast forward seven years later from our first session and I was still taking lessons with Sonny. I learned so much from that man, from day one to the last session we had; from holding a stick and striking the drum properly to reading big band jazz chart music. He opened up so much potential in my playing abilities and I grew and learned so much about music and about life in general. Here was an 80-year-old man who, when behind the kit, played like he was in his 20s. He was filled with so much knowledge and insight about the drums that I never thought I'd learn as much as I did from him that first time we met.

Mentor

In life we all try to find someone who we can look up to and learn more from. In my case, I had and still have the opportunity to learn from the best, my father. I remember the day I made the decision I wanted to become a plumbing contractor. I'll never forget his words, "Plumbing is the easy part. Knowing how to deal with customers is the hard part." My father is not one to literally sit with someone and show them how to do certain plumbing tasks. However, he is someone you can learn from just by watching and observing his techniques and the way he speaks and handles plumbing situations and customers. I've learned so much from my father about business and about life. There are times that I still think I know more than he does when it comes to plumbing, but then I'm quickly reminded that I still have a lot to learn. I try to keep an open mind when I'm working out in the field every day and I try to soak up as much information as possible. Become open minded. During the end of that lesson I had with Vinney, I thought I had learned everything I needed to know about drumming and that there was no one out there who could teach me quite as well as he did. I quickly shot down the idea of reaching out and learning from an 80-year-old jazz guy. Good thing I had a change in heart and decided not to box myself in and become closed minded. I learned so much from Sonny, not only with my rudiments and reading of big band music, but about life in general. Whoever it is you look up to and learn from, it is important to never think you know it all and that there is always room for improvement in life and in business. You must learn to adapt to change and be open minded to learning from others. Either you look up to someone older than you or you may look up to someone who is younger than you. Regardless of who it is or how old he or she is, you must keep an open mind. Never box yourself in! Let me know who your mentor is in your life. Please email me.

Dominate Your Dance

"Mama! Dada! It's Christmas morning! It's Christmas morning!" Mason screamed at the top of his lungs at 6a.m. at the foot of our bed. I opened my one eye and shot my wife Azure that look. "It can't be morning already," I mumbled under my breath. Before I could open up my other eye, Mason and I were nose to nose as he said, "Dada, are you awake? Are you awake yet?" I laughed and replied, "Yes, Mason, I am awake." My wife and I proceeded to give each other a kiss and hugged and kissed Mason and Norman and wished each of them a Merry Christmas. Before we knew it, we were covered in wrapping paper, loud toys, tape and bulldog drool as Norman loved tearing up all that paper.

"Mason, I can't believe Santa gave you all of these gifts!" I said. "I know Dada, I must have been good to deserve all of these toys!" he replied. I looked at my wife and gave her the "that's debatable" look. "Dada, where's Mama's gift? Was she good enough like me to get a gift?" Mason asked. I began to laugh and responded, "I think she's been good. What do you think?" Mason nodded with excitement. "Well I didn't get a chance to wrap her gift so why don't I whisper in your ear and then you can tell her what the gift is," I said. Mason then ran over and threw his head into my nose and began to whisper, "Okay, tell me." I then whispered into his ear and his eyes lit up with excitement. He ran over to Azure, whispered into her ear and the tears began to flow from my wife's face... Was it a car? A trip to Bermuda? A Spa getaway? Nope. While those would also create tears of joy, this gift was, believe it or not, right up there with the above options. "Oh my god, Sean, really? Dancing with the Stars Live tour tickets!?" I smiled from ear to ear and gave her a hug. Making her happy is one of the greatest feelings. "But who will watch Mason for us?" she quickly asked. "Don't worry. I got it covered..."

Of course, the night of the show, I got stuck on a job. If it could go wrong, it certainly did! I managed to finish up the heater and raced home in order to get to the show in plenty of time. I took one of the quickest showers and threw on some clothes. Next thing, the doorbell rang and it was one of Mason's uncles, my younger brother, Brendan. Mason went bonkers, jumping up and down, running left and right showing him all of his new toys from Santa. We gave Brendan the thumbs up and snuck out the door, excited for our date night out.

After a wonderful dinner and a few Grey Goose martinis in me, we made our way into the theater for the Dancing with the Stars show. I got some snacks, drinks and a show program for my wife. We found our seats and the show began! As I looked around, I began to notice that almost every woman in the theater had a boyfriend or husband right by their side. Each of the women were smiling and glowing from ear to ear. As for the men, they looked on, trying not show too much excitement, because they wouldn't want to appear "interested" in a "dancing show." I quietly laughed to myself and looked to my wife as her smile was still stuck in place.

I then turned my focus back to the stage as my attention was quickly captured by this one dancer. She came out onto the stage and she demanded the attention through her unbelievable talent. I don't know much about dancing, but when this woman stepped onto the stage, she owned the dance floor! Confidence, drive, passion, determination are just a few words to describe her and her dancing abilities. Our seats were not the best, as they were a good distance from the stage, but I knew immediately when she was off and/or on the stage. I then leaned over to my wife and whispered, "Who is that up there?" She knew exactly who I was talking about and answered immediately, "Jenna Johnson." I nodded and said, "She's incredible!" She looked at me with that surprised but satisfied look on her face that I was paying attention and seemed to be enjoying myself. As I watched throughout the evening, I quickly became inspired by Jenna Johnson's skills and passion and I knew exactly what I was going to write for my next chapter.

Should I? Shouldn't I? I kept debating whether or not I should write a chapter about my experience at a DWTS show. Well, as you can tell, I've decided to write about it! But why? - If you take a look at people like Jenna and how she's become so successful in her industry, it's most likely because of her hard work, passion, drive, dedication, love and determination for becoming the best dancer in her space. Well, the same applies for our industry.

As you read this chapter, I don't care if you are a plumber or not, you should learn something from this piece. To get noticed out there and become the best at what you do, you must apply the hard work, passion, creativity, drive and love for your skill or trade. I am driven every day to run the most successful plumbing business in my region. My goal is to dominate my space, in my plumbing business, writing, product development, etc. Whatever it is for you, take action and demand the attention you deserve. You must become obsessed with whatever it is you want to become extremely successful in. To help keep me motivated throughout the day, I created an inspiration band for myself that I wear everyday around my wrist and it reads, "Dominate Your Space." It's a friendly reminder to keep me motivated and driven to be the best in my sector.

Find whatever it is for you that gets you motivated; it very well may be this book. For me, it was that Tuesday evening being blown away and inspired by a dancer! It may be a book, article, music, athlete or something or someone you may never have thought would motivate you. But however you get motivated, take the feeling, harness it and take action. I hope enjoyed this book and that it has ignited a fire within you to go out there and dominate the dance of your life!

www.ingramcontent.com/pod-product-compliance
Lightning Source LLC
Chambersburg PA
CBHW032002190326
41520CB00007B/323